McGraw-Hill's

WRITING AN OUTSTANDING COLLEGE APPLICATION ESSAY

McGraw-Hill's

WRITING AN OUTSTANDING COLLEGE APPLICATION ESSAY

ESTELLE RANKIN
BARBARA MURPHY

McGraw-Hill

NEW YORK | CHICAGO | SAN FRANCISCO | LISBON
LONDON | MADRID | MEXICO CITY | MILAN | NEW DELHI
SAN JUAN | SEOUL | SINGAPORE | SYDNEY | TORONTO

The *McGraw·Hill* Companies

2 3 4 5 6 7 8 9 0   DOC/DOC   0 9 8 7 6 5

ISBN 0-07-144813-6

McGraw-Hill books are available at special quantity discounts to use as premiums and sales promotions, or for use in corporate training programs. For more information, please write to the Director of Special Sales, Professional Publishing, McGraw-Hill, Two Penn Plaza, New York, NY 10121-2298. Or contact your local bookstore.

 This book is printed on recycled, acid-free paper containing a minimum of 50% recycled, de-inked fiber.

CONTENTS

ACKNOWLEDGMENTS

♥ Our love and appreciation to Allan and Leah for their constant support and encouragement. Our very special thanks to the many students throughout the United States who were so gracious and cooperative in granting us access to their thoughts and ideas as expressed in their college application essays, and to their teachers and parents who have nurtured these astute and thoughtful young people.

We particularly would like to acknowledge the following educators: Dr. Scott Andrews, principal of Amityville High School; Diane Antonucci, Jericho High School English instructor; Wan Chen, Hempstead High School English instructor; James Dazenski, Great Neck South High School English chairperson; Dr. Sandi Forsythe, Green Valley High School English instructor; Dr. Thomas Ganes, Great Neck South High School director of guidance; Dr. Louisa Kramer-Vida, Oyster Bay District English coordinator; Dr. Irene McKenna, California State University Emeritus Professor of Comparative Literature; Karen Meier, Patchogue-Medford director of English and Reading; Allison Moran, Massapequa High School guidance counselor; Claire Paccione, Bellmore-Merrick English chairperson; Kathi Reilly, Oyster Bay English coordinator; Joan Rosenberg, Jericho High School guidance counselor; Randy Rosenberg, Cornell University admissions interviewer; Dr. Charlotte Rosenzwieg, Long Beach District Language Arts coordinator; John Schmitt, Massapequa English instructor; Dr. Lois Smith, Jericho High School director of guidance; Lyn Tise, Patchogue-Medford High School English instructor; Martha Wheelock, Harvard Westlake School English instructor; and Dr. Nina Wolff, educational consultant for the Bay Shore college admissions program.

The following students were willing to be risk takers in allowing their writing to be incorporated into the pages of this book. They, and all of our other students, are the primary reason why all of us do the work we do.

Ari Allen
Kari Andersen
Rachel Beller
Stephanie Bragman
Erin Brown
Neil Chen
Tarnjit Devi
Nicole Duke
Rebecca Frank
Lara Friedrich
Jessica Frumer
Timothy Gill
Rebecca Gitlin
Karin Hoesl
Saira Hussain

Allison Ivans
Julie Kaplan
Kathleen Kenary
Brendan Kennedy
Danielle Labadorf
Arielle Laurie
Earle Le Masters IV
Kat Lewin
Grace Lin
Chrissy Makris
Meredith Maus
Sean K. Mehra
Jeanne Messerschmitt
Heather Nathan
Brooke Nielsen

Ashley Peterson
Elyse Pieper
Christine Poynter
Jeremy Price
Josh Putterman
Jessica Restivo
Jake Rosenblum
Michala Smith
Joelle Soliman
Kaveh Tabatabaie
Ashleigh Tate
Nicole Tsourovakas
Dana Van Pamelen
Virginia Viviano
Hillary Wissemann

The following high schools are represented:

☑ Bay Shore High School, Bayshore, New York

☑ Great Neck South High School, Great Neck, New York

☑ Green Valley High School, Henderson, Nevada

☑ Harvard-Westlake School, North Hollywood, California

☑ Hempstead High School, Hempstead, New York

☑ Jericho High School, Jericho, New York

☑ Massapequa High School, Massapequa, New York

☑ Mepham High School, Bellmore-Merrick, New York

☑ Oyster Bay High School, Oyster Bay, New York

☑ Patchogue-Medford High School, Patchogue-Medford, New York

McGraw-Hill's

WRITING AN OUTSTANDING COLLEGE APPLICATION ESSAY

INTRODUCING THE COLLEGE APPLICATION ESSAY

This year close to 2 million students will apply for freshman admission[1] to over 2,300 four-year colleges and universities in the United States.[2] At first glance, the numbers appear overwhelming. And here you are—transcript in hand, four years of your life reduced to a series of numbers and columns on a digitized, impersonal sheet of paper. How will college admissions officers ever know to pick you; how will they ever know who you really are and how much you want to go to their college?

We are not going to say, "Relax." On the contrary, we are very much aware that this IS a very stressful time for you. In many ways, it is a matter of all or nothing.

Some of you have your hearts set on a particular school, some of you have no idea where you want to go, and some of you have known since childhood exactly what your calling is, while others will be searching their entire lives. But one thing is certain; you all have one thing in common: ALL of you must write the college application essay.

---

[1]David A. Hawkins and Jessica Lantz, *The State of College Admissions*, The National Association for College Admission Counseling, March 2005, p. 9.
[2]"Our First Annual College-Admissions Survey," *The Atlantic Monthly*, November 2003, www.the atlantic.com/issues/2003/11/admissions.htm.

Do not despair. We are here to guide you through the maze that is the college application essay process. That's right—you who are the dreamers and the schemers. You who are the scholars and the athletes, the artists and the scientists, the idealists and the pragmatists. You who are the wonderers and the wanderers. Each of you is unique. Your take on your world is yours alone, yours now to share and explore with the colleges of your choice.

The moment your college application essay is read by the admissions committee, you alone take center stage. We will help you choose your part, rehearse your lines, and accept the applause. We will provide you with models and activities that will allow you to both observe the process at work and become involved in each step of the process.

Let's begin.

FREQUENTLY ASKED QUESTIONS
What is a college application essay?

The college application essay is your personal introduction to the school to which you are applying. You are putting yourself into the direct gaze of the admissions committee. It's a blind date, and your job is to make the committee want to ask you out again. But the application essay has other purposes as well. It also reveals:

- ☑ Your thoughts about a selected topic
- ☑ Something about your interests and insights
- ☑ Your readiness for the challenges afforded by the college
- ☑ Your self-awareness and achievements
- ☑ Your goals and challenges
- ☑ Your academic strengths
- ☑ Your "compatibility" with the college
- ☑ Your attitude toward yourself and your world
- ☑ Your creativity
- ☑ Your passion(s)

And as if this weren't enough, the admissions people will also be looking at your writing ability, and that includes:

- ☑ Facility with language
- ☑ Organizational skills
- ☑ The ability to create and support a central thesis
- ☑ Mechanics and vocabulary
- ☑ Syntax
- ☑ Proofreading skills
- ☑ Revision skills

What do the colleges expect in the essay?

The colleges expect final drafts that respond to the question asked. They expect essays that are:

- ☑ Authentic to the writer
- ☑ Engaging
- ☑ Suitable for a college-level student
- ☑ Indicative of potential for success at the particular college

Will I have a choice of questions?

Yes. Colleges are not looking to pigeonhole you or to hamper your creativity. The variety of questions will provide some parameters within which you can choose a way to introduce yourself. Even if you're given a single question, it will be open-ended enough to allow you to choose your point of view and to present it with your own personal twist. See Chapter 3.

I don't know where to start? How do I choose a topic?

That's easy. Turn to Chapter 3. We'll lead you through a series of activities that will reacquaint *you* with you. There's so much about you that you don't even remember, and the work you do in this chapter will help jog your memory so that you will have a storehouse of material from which to draw.

My strength is math and science. Am I at a disadvantage when it comes to writing this essay?

No, provided that your essay is a clear, sincere, polished response to the question and manages to convey a sense of who *you* are.

Is my essay going to be graded?

Graded, no, but it is certainly going to be evaluated. Let's be honest. **The essay that has spelling and grammar errors, that is poorly organized with many clichés and childish phrases, is not going to be well received.**

Can I be funny?

If you choose to use humor, make certain it is because it's natural for you to be funny and you're comfortable with some of the techniques of humor. You know what your own response is to a joke that you don't get or don't find funny. The same holds true for the admissions staff. **Do not try to force a laugh. And by all means, avoid being cutesy.**

On the other hand, don't feel that you must be ponderous or overly serious. **Feel free to include amusing anecdotes, light-hearted asides, puns, banter, etc., *if* it is suitable and appropriate for both you and your topic.** For further information, see Chapter 4.

What happens if I write less than or more than the number of words that they ask for?

We're talking here about the essay that runs, for example, 900 words or 250 words rather than the assigned 500. The reader's first impression of you is that you don't, won't, or can't follow directions. This is certainly not an impression that we advise you to give. (See Chapter 5 on evaluating your first draft.)

However, we are not saying that you must count every single word. Do not sacrifice the impact of your essay to strictly adhere to the word count. Be reasonable and discriminating and stay as close as possible to the college's particular guidelines.

Should I have other people read my essay?

Yes, without a doubt; this is a must! And we recommend that they read it out loud to *you*. But, remember, it's your essay, not theirs: not your mother's, your teacher's, your friend's, your tutor's. They can all read what you've written and respond to it, but they are NOT the author. *You* are. Use others to see and hear what sections are effective, what questions need to be addressed, what sentences or phrases do not read well. **Let their readings and reactions be your guide to what works and what doesn't work, what needs to be dropped and what needs to be added.** Make it your own.

How much does the essay count in the admissions process?

Trust us, it counts. While there is no single mathematical formula for weighting the essay, it is certainly a major determining factor in the acceptance process. If you are applying to a highly competitive school, it is safe to assume that the other applicants are just as proficient and well rounded as you. (One student, a valedictorian accepted at an Ivy League school, was amazed to discover that nearly every classmate in his English class also had been a high school valedictorian.) **Since grades, scores, and activities are fairly objective information, it falls to the essay to separate one bright student from another.**

If you are a strong student who writes an exceptional paper, you have absolutely increased your chances of acceptance. If, on the other hand, you are a strong student who writes a weak paper, you are likely to fall a notch in the eyes of the admissions committee.

What shouldn't I write about?

Bear in mind that certain topics are difficult to assess objectively: divorce, tragedies, physical ailments, and disabilities. These subjects are very real, very personal, and very emotional. Often the retelling of the circumstances tends to be so universally touching that it leaves little or no room for the admissions reader to determine your suitability for acceptance to college. If you do refer to a sensitive issue or situation, remember to use it as a vehicle to move your presentation to a more unique perspective about yourself.

Controversial topics can also present problems to the admissions reader. The application essay is your personal introduction: it is NOT a forum for political diatribes or religious preaching. Remember that an emphasis on blame, negativity, and use of hateful language may reveal a side of you that you would not want to be considered in the application process.

That being said, make certain to take a look at Chapter 6, which deals with writers who dare to take risks when writing their application essays. Guide yourself accordingly.

Can I use an essay I've previously written for a school assignment?

Our instinct is to say NO for the following reasons:

1. The essay was in response to a very specific academic situation (e.g., Shakespeare's love sonnets, leadership at the Yalta Conference). While your thoughts and writing may be excellent, the essay will probably not reveal much about you.

2. The voice you use for the academic essay is usually not the voice you want to use when introducing yourself to your college. One is formal and analytical; the other is informal and personal.

3. Some colleges offer you the opportunity to include extra evidence of your achievements and potential. In fact, some may even ask for a paper with your teacher's comments on it. In such a case, you can definitely submit your academic essay. But it is NOT a replacement for your personal application essay.

Keep the essay readily accessible because you may be able to utilize an idea or a quotation from it in your application essay.

A DISCUSSION WITH THE EXPERTS

In addition to your own apprehensions, you must be wondering if you are alone in the process. This is a stressful time for you, for your parents, and for your teachers and guidance counselors. Everyone is giving advice, and you're not sure if it's the advice you really need. In the previous section of this chapter, you read responses to frequently asked questions, and the answers to those queries are the result of our experience and research.

However, it's human nature to ask, "Is that all there is?" No, and to further enlighten you on your quest, we have gathered together a group of experts, all of whom are very well versed in the college application process. We invite you to join us in a roundtable discussion concerning common questions, practices, and advice regarding the college application essay. We're certain that by the end of this discussion, many of your questions will have been addressed. The members of our panel are:

Dr. Scott Andrews, principal of Amityville High School, former director of guidance at Mineola High School

Dr. Thomas Ganes, director of guidance, Great Neck South High School

Dr. Irene McKenna, emeritus professor of comparative literature, California State University at Dominguez Hills

Joan Rosenberg, guidance counselor, Jericho High School guidance counselor

Randy Rosenberg, admissions interviewer, Cornell University

Dr. Lois Smith, director of guidance, Jericho High School

Nina Wolff, educational consultant; created the Bay Shore College Admissions Tutorial Program; former director of English/language arts for Bay Shore schools

Pull up a chair and join us as we discuss issues that are common to us all.

Let's begin this roundtable with one of the most obvious areas of concern:

Can the college application essay be the deciding factor?

"Absolutely. It's very important because it demonstrates a student's expressive language, and we have several readers consider it if there is a doubt about the applicant's qualification for admission" (R. Rosenberg). "I, too, think the essay is quite important, and it may even be a deciding factor in admission to private schools, like Smith and Mount Holyoke" (I. McKenna)

How early should one begin to think about college applications?

"We begin in January of the junior year when we bring in college admissions personnel" (T. Ganes). "In ninth grade we provide the Common Application to parents. In tenth grade, we offer a college prep writing course" (J. Rosenberg). "All students should be provided with college awareness, beginning in middle school. It's incumbent upon low-income/high-need districts to instill college awareness and the belief that college/university is a reachable goal for all. Our English teachers utilize the Common Application essays in class to help give our students a jump-start on the college application process" (S. Andrews).

From your experience who is involved in writing the application essay?

"We ask our students to show their essay to their English teacher prior to submission. The counselors will also read the essays and give the students feedback. It's our hope that parents will also take an active role and look at the essay. We frequently speak with the college admissions representatives and get advice and guidelines from them, which we pass on to the students" (L. Smith). "We follow the same policy; teachers and counselors read essays. English teachers review student essays at the request of students in one-on-one writing conferences" (T. Ganes). "In addition to the English teachers and counselors, business teachers may also read the essays" (S. Andrews). "We offer a consortium of retired English teachers who conduct private tutorial sessions in order to help students tackle the difficult task of writing college admissions essays" (N. Wolff). "Students need guidance, but you can tell when the student has not written any part of an essay. I prefer the voice of the student even if she makes mistakes" (I. McKenna)

What do you look for in the application essay?

"A good beginning—an attention-getter. Follow-through. Well-organized ideas ending in a clever, memorable manner" (I. McKenna). "I agree. Write a catchy opening that gets right to the point with specific, personal details that stress your thesis; and write a catchy closing that brings a smile to the face of the admission's officer and makes your essay unforgettable" (N. Wolff). "We look for an articulation of the match between experience and the chosen field of study" (R. Rosenberg). "Personally, I like a witty essay rather than a humorous essay. If the student knows the difference between the two, she's on solid ground" (I. McKenna). "Use your own voice; the essay must sound as if a teenager has written it" (N. Wolff).

Is there anything that turns you off in an essay?

"Yes—a sentence such as 'My academic transcript speaks for itself'" (R. Rosenberg). "Laundry lists of activities they've participated in" (N. Wolff). "I don't like essays that follow a form, such as, 'In this essay I will...'" (I. McKenna). "A mindset that says, 'We'll make it fit.' Being lazy, and trying to use an essay from another assignment" (J. Rosenberg).

What about controversial subjects?

"I think I respond well, but that's my opinion. I believe we all think we respond well, but we often don't. Consequently, controversy should be left to essays written after the student is admitted; then, she will know her audience. I would also say that essays on a religious or political theme can be off-putting" (I. McKenna). "We ask our students to consider the following: Does it answer the question? Is it too far out in left field? Is it offensive to anyone? Could it be misinterpreted?" (J. Rosenberg). "Controversy is very subjective and a topic that has to be dealt with carefully. Some students are more willing to take risks in their essays, and if they are comfortable with it, you need to be open and honest; but never say they should not submit it" (T. Ganes). "If an essay seems inappropriate or doesn't really answer the question, we suggest that they might want to take a different approach with their answer" (L. Smith).

What are your general recommendations for the student who is about to write his or her application essay?

"Follow directions! Pay attention to the recommended length; start early and revise several times" (J. Rosenberg). "Don't try to overly impress the college representatives. Be real. Tell your story from your point of view" (S. Andrews). "I read essays for the CSU English entrance exam—to place students in regular or developmental classes. Long essays, after you've read fifty, are not appreciated" (I. McKenna). " I agree. 'Brevity is the soul of wit.' Do some surgery on the piece. Edit for sentence variety, and make sure each paragraph has a topic sentence that relates back to your introduction or thesis statement. Read your piece aloud to check for awkward phrases that could slow down or confuse the reader" (N. Wolff). "Be as concise as possible and consider what the reader learns about you after he/she reads the essay" (T. Ganes). "As part of my top ten list, I recommend that students come up with an original idea; use specific details, anecdotes; and proofread for errors in grammar and punctuation. I also stress relevance. Make sure that the essay makes a connection to college" (N. Wolff).

Do you have any final points you would like to make to the students who will be reading this book?

"Be yourself!" (T. Ganes). "Our parents and students are basically concerned with the increasing competitiveness of many of the colleges they would like to attend. We encourage them to write essays that are truly 'genuine.' My biggest pointer for students is to start early in the process and be organized" (L. Smith). "Write from your heart. Explain how you were impacted by a particular life experience. Own the essay. Do not try to get into the reader's mind. Be honest. No fluff" (S. Andrews). "Be specific. Don't write what you think they want to hear. Write your own essay. Be passionate. Be a seventeen-year-old!" (J. Rosenberg).

"When my niece applied to colleges, we discussed her essay. I told her to think about her interests and strengths. At the time, she was the catcher on her high school softball team. We talked about what she did as a catcher, what decisions she had to make, how she made them, and how she felt when she succeeded or failed. She used her catcher's experience as a metaphor for her life experiences. This idea worked very well for her. She's a Smith graduate.

"When my sister applied for a master's program, she agonized about writing her admissions essay. She claimed she had no talents. I told her to come up with one sentence that would make her 'understood' or 'known' to a person she had never met. Hours later, she told me, 'I don't know what to say. The only thing I can think of is "Children and dogs like me."' What a great sentence! If you met Amy, you would know that just about says it. As a teacher, I like to have students communicate their voices by having them think about engaging their audience. For example, if you were at a party, what would you say about yourself to a person you wished to get to know?" (I. McKenna).

"Look at writing the college admissions essay not as a chore but as an interesting journey into your soul. What have you gained from your education and experiences? How have you matured? What are your goals and dreams? Whom have you met along the way? It's important to reflect on these questions before entering the next phase: college and beyond!" (N. Wolff).

HOW TO USE THIS BOOK
For the Ordered, Structured Writer

You know who you are. You are an ordered, structured writer if you:

      ☑ Bought this book in your junior year

      ☑ Like to make lists and keep calendars

☑ Keep notes, files, journals, notebooks, etc.

☑ Are comfortable meeting tasks on time or even early

☑ Are comfortable working in stages

☑ Enjoy revision

If this describes you, the following could prove to be a usable plan for the application essay process.

☑ Google your colleges and look at their Web sites and essay prompts.

☑ By the second half of your junior year:

➤ Collect all of your "notes" into one place.

➤ Establish a college file.

➤ Get an overview of this book and its approach.

➤ Using the table of contents as your guide, spread out the application essay process over the next several months.

☑ Set a goal to return to school as a senior with the rough draft of your college application essay already completed.

For the Creative Writer

You're a creative writer if you:

☑ Love words

☑ Love to read

☑ Like to say things differently from others

☑ Are comfortable with emotions, description, and/or experimentation

For those of you who recognize yourselves as creative writers, one of your major challenges will be to limit yourself. To this end,

☑ We suggest you go to Chapter 2 of this book and have a wild and wacky time conducting your personal interview and completing the brainstorming activities. Feel free to experiment.

☑ Your challenge will be to choose that ONE topic that will allow you to be yourself, express yourself, and reveal yourself as the unique individual you are while LIMITING yourself to the purpose, audience, and prescribed length.

☑ You may want to submit different essays to different colleges. You don't have to limit yourself to just one generic essay.

For the Reluctant Writer

Do the following describe you?

☑ Writing the application essay is an unpleasant, stressful obligation.

☑ English may not be your strongest subject.

☑ You're afraid to put words down on paper.

☑ You assume you have nothing to say.

Relax. You're not alone. This book will provide you with an accessible, user-friendly process for writing your application essay. We know you have something unique to present.

☑ Start at the very beginning of this book. Work your way through the book with us. We'll be with you during every step of the process. We've broken the process into small pieces for you—pieces that you can easily handle.

☑ We encourage you to relax and have some fun. You will be writing about something you know well. And once you get started, the organization and details will fall into place.

☑ You may want to talk through your ideas with someone you trust BEFORE even beginning to write down anything.

For the Writer Who Works Best under Pressure

The writer who seems to work best under pressure believes that:

- ☑ The last possible moment is the right time to begin writing.
- ☑ November 30 is a great time to begin writing a paper due on December 1.
- ☑ Pressure really works.

Don't panic. We are not going to try to change you. But...now, hear this!

- ☑ If the deadline is December 1, set the due date back at least three days to November 27. Play this game with us, please. Give yourself a break. You do need at least some time to reflect, edit, proofread, and revise. You need a little distance. Three days is a minimum.
- ☑ *Don't skip Chapter 2 of this book.*
- ☑ Make certain to read the sample student essays and commentaries to get an idea of the wide variety of approaches to writing and and the wide range of levels of the application essay.

ABOUT THE ORGANIZATION AND GRAPHICS

This book is organized to provide you with the best opportunity to gather information about the college application essay from the point of view of both experts and students. We have arranged Chapters 2, 3, 4, and 5 into sections that introduce you to an idea or process, provide examples of this process for you, and give you a chance to practice with the process.

Points that we feel are of **special importance will be highlighted in bold print.** Some may also have a ➡ beside them. To take you through the writing process, we will introduce you to two writers whose names are **Elvira** 👱 and **Jake** 🧑. These two writers will actually work through each writing activity. In the sections titled **WORKING WITH OUR TWO WRITERS**, you will read their essays and the comments as they complete each activity. And following their examples, you will have your own opportunity, ☞ **YOUR TURN** ☜, to write each section of your own essay. If you follow our process, by the end of this book you will have a well-written college application essay ready to mail to the college or university of your choice.

ONE FINAL POINT: You have been in English classes for well over 10 years; therefore, we are *not* here to teach you grammar or tell you how to write an essay. We *are* here to guide you through the process and to point out areas that you may need to consider and monitor as you think about, plan, write, and evaluate your college application essay.

EXAMINING YOUR LIFE
AND FINDING YOUR PASSION

"Help! I'm just ordinary."
"Nothing ever happens to me."
"I don't even know who I am. How can I tell them?"
"Boring. That's what they're going to think—boring."

Sound familiar? Well, we have a news flash for you. You ARE interesting. You have had many unique experiences. And with some honest answers to a few questions, you are going to be amazed by how much you have to say about yourself.

What we propose is a personal interview. Here's the hook. This interview is with yourself, *by* yourself. What follows is a random list of categories that we want you to fill in with specifics. We've mixed the list up so that you can think and answer in clusters, intuitive responses, or spontaneous reactions. This is the fun part. Be loose; pull out the stops; brag; exaggerate; be witty, serious, clever, academic. Let your mind free-associate as you brainstorm. Don't just give one-word answers. Search for the potential in your answers. Feel free to add to the list or to modify it to suit your needs. Come back to the list—let it percolate in your brain. We guarantee that by the time you've worked your way through the interview, you will have many, many ideas for your college essay. Remember, your responses are a springboard to more fully developed explanations. This should be an enjoyable activity that tickles your memory and challenges you a little bit. Don't be afraid to tell the truth. This is how you find **your voice.**

Your Very Own Personal Interview

To get into the spirit of this "personal interview" scenario, you're going to need a pad, a notebook, a stack of index cards, or a sheaf of paper. Or if you prefer, you might even want to respond to these in a file you set up on your computer titled "My Personal Interview."

☑ Think about the topics.

☑ Talk to yourself.

☑ Brainstorm.

☑ Make a copy of this list and keep it in your bedroom, in your bathroom, in your locker, or on your computer's desktop.

☑ Add to this list.

The list will help you combat writer's block and make you aware of how interesting and unique you really are.

To give you an idea of how this process works, take a look at how our two students, **Elvira** and **Jake**, constructed their own lists. Elvira's responses are in *italics* and Jake's are in **bold.**

If I could change one thing:	*my being unable to sleep*	**world hunger**
My goals are:	*BORING*	**X**
My favorite movie(s) is: (why?)	*X*	***The Producers, Citizen Kane***
I wish I knew... (person or character)	*X*	**Abraham Lincoln**
I wish I knew... (ideas)	*how to be more organized*	**X**
I can't live without:	*Haagen Däz haha!*	**X**

The greatest thrill for me would be:	*X*	**X**
The song that moves me most is: (why?)	*X*	**too many to remember, always changing**
My dream job would be:	*X*	**X**
A pet story or memory:	*Laddie & the corned beef sandwich disaster*	**X**
A unique talent I have:	*playing alphabet categories*	**X**
Something I'm ashamed of is:	*a disaster with my hair*	**X**
Best friends or old friends or lost friends or new friends:	*X*	**never mind**
Colors in my life:	*yuck!*	**X**
The greatest gadget:	*X*	**X**
A secret desire I have is:	*X*	**to climb Mt. Everest**
The most moving thing I ever read or heard or saw is:	*X*	**X**
The best of times:	*prom night*	**winning the championship**
The worst of times:	*9/11*	**too hard to think about**
Rituals:	*my family ordering dinner in a restaurant*	**X**
The things or people that make me laugh:	*X*	**too much**

A practical joke:	*friends like to play them on me*	**forget it**
A disaster (comic or real or imagined):	*dyeing my hair pink*	**X**
Driving	*X*	**my first car accident**
Temptation (avoided or given in to):	*X*	**X**
The things or people that make me cry:	*X*	**X**
Things that fill me with wonder:	*X*	**mountains**
What a character!	*Aunt Pip. tea & crumpets & Scrabble*	**X**
My unsung hero:	*X*	**X**
I'm so frustrated by:	*this whole sleeping process!*	**X**
The best thing I ever learned:	*X*	**to respect differences**
First loves:	*X*	**I don't want to talk about it.**
I'm outraged by:	*hunger in America*	**lies politicians tell**
I have to change:	*my socks*	**X**
My favorite paintings or artists are:	*Degas' Ballerina*	**Ansel Adams**
My secret haunt:	*X*	**X**
A time period I wish I had lived in and why:	*X*	**X**
The best book I've read this year is: (why)	*Harry Potter*	***The DaVinci Code***

I'm proudest of:	*X*	**making Mrs. Crenshaw smile**
I'd like to meet:	*Sharon Olds, Maya Angelou*	**Stephen King, Tiger Woods**
Don't ask me to...	*go to bed early*	**X**
An ethical dilemma I faced:	*X*	**cheating on 6th grade science test**
An injustice:	*X*	**world hunger**
I did it!	*X*	**good for you!**
There will never be another...	*X*	**X**
I'm a survivor:	*of ballet lessons*	**of Coach Bender's practices**
The joys of nature:	*X*	**X**
A challenge I met:	*X*	**learning to make good foul shots**
Something I hated... until:	*broccoli*	**classical music**
My favorite place on earth:	*X*	**X**
My creed or I believe:	*too personal*	**it'll sound corny**
I won't part with:	*my grandmother's ring*	**my grandfather's pen**
Just once I'd like to:	*fall asleep quickly*	**X**
I soar when...	*X*	**X**
An opinion I changed and why:	*X*	**old people don't really interest me**
Sports and me—what a team:	*tennis*	**basketball**
I love...	*X*	**the movies**

Words I love:	*snow day*	**yes**
Words I hate:	*X*	**no**
The greatest gift:	*X*	**X**
An emotional tug of war:	*X*	**X**
The weakest link:	*X*	**X**
Stick with me kid, I'm going places:	*X*	**X**
Most people don't know this, but I'm...	*an insomniac*	**X**
Food, glorious food:	*X*	**I love fast food no matter what others say**
But you can't choose your family... or can you?	*X*	**X**
My road not taken:	*X*	**X**
The sweetest sounds I ever heard:	*X*	**X**
Time is on my side because:	*X*	**X**
Not all lessons are in class:	*X*	**X**
I took a chance:	*X*	**telling my friends that we have to stop making fun of a teacher**
I get a kick out of:	*finishing this*	**X**
I need...	*X*	**to be done with this!**

This is a sample of how two students notated their lists. Elvira and Jake marked an X next to those questions where they couldn't come up with a response right away. They'll come back to the list periodically, filling in blanks until they have a complete set of ideas to work from. You see—it's simple. Just let yourself feel free. Go with your first responses. It can be liberating.

☞ YOUR TURN ☜

BEGIN HERE:

If I could change one thing: _____

My goals are: _____

My favorite movie(s) is: (why?) _____

I wish I knew... (person or character) _____

I wish I knew... (ideas) _____

I can't live without: _____

The greatest thrill for me would be: _____

The song that moves me most is: (why?) _____

My dream job would be: _____

A pet story or memory: _____

A unique talent I have: _____

Something I'm ashamed of is: _____

Best friends or old friends or lost friends or new friends: _____

Colors in my life: _____

The greatest gadget: _____

A secret desire I have is: _____

The most moving thing I ever read or heard or saw is: _____

The best of times: _____

The worst of times: _____

Rituals: _____

The things or people that make me laugh: _____

A practical joke: _____

A disaster (comic or real or imagined): _____

Driving: _____

Temptation (avoided or given in to): _____

The things or people that make me cry: _____

Things that fill me with wonder: _____

What a character!_____

My unsung hero: _____

I'm so frustrated by: _____

The best thing I ever learned:_____

First loves: _____

I'm outraged by:_____

I have to change: _____

My favorite paintings or artists are: _____

My secret haunt: _____

A time period I wish I had lived in and why: _____

The best book I've read this year is: (why) _____

I'm proudest of: _____

I'd like to meet: _____

Don't ask me to... _____

An ethical dilemma I faced: _____

An injustice:_____

I did it! _____

There will never be another... _____

I'm a survivor: _____

The joys of nature:_____

A challenge I met: _____

Something I hated...until: _____

My favorite place on earth: _____

My creed or I believe: _____

I won't part with: _____

Just once I'd like to: _____

I soar when... _____

An opinion I changed and why: _____

Sports and me—what a team: _____

I love... _____

Words I love: _____

Words I hate: _____

The greatest gift: _____

An emotional tug of war: _____

The weakest link: _____

Stick with me kid, I'm going places: _____

Most people don't know this, but I'm... _____

Food, glorious food: _____

But you can't choose your family... or can you? _____

My road not taken: _____

The sweetest sounds I ever heard: _____

Time is on my side because: _____

Not all lessons are in class: _____

I took a chance: _____

I get a kick out of: _____

I need... _____

Well, do you feel you "know thyself"? We bet you know more about yourself than you realized. And, of course, this is an exercise you can do anywhere, anytime, with multiple repetitions and an entirely different set of answers. Up the ante—play with the list in a humorous vein. Then change and provide serious answers for the queries. Change again and try to fill it out for someone else. The goal here is to have you consider the possibilities of those experiences you can use in an application essay to suit various types of questions.

The Brainstorming Process

To give you an idea of the brainstorming process, consider the following models that are random responses to six of the items on the list. These notes were hand-written on a sheet of paper in five minutes. THAT IS ALL THE TIME IT TOOK. Keep in mind that these are spontaneous responses and, therefore, rough, fresh, and not overworked. They are "as is."

Sample 1: Most people don't know this, but I'm...an insomniac!

Bed, bed, I couldn't get to sleep
Now, I lay me down to sleep—
I don't think so!

bedtime starts with: *Friends*, *Frasier*,
   Food Network
Moves to: alphabet games:
    Indian tribes—Arapaho to Zuni
    26 shades of blue—cerulean & Prussian
Then, I move to colors derived from fruits—thank heaven for kiwi.
   ➜ after that fails—educational T.V.—channel 49
Too much to know; life is too full to close my eyes.

Hope to sleep by morning
My mind races—reads for a while,
but the book gets heavy & my neck hurts

I think... I think...

> **Sample 2: My favorite movies are:**
>
> *The Producers—* absurd, belly laughs, love Zero Mostel and Gene Wilder
> *Citizen Kane—* THE best of all. The idea of absolute power corrupting absolutely
> *Casablanca—* Love and adventure
> *Some Like It Hot—* Just plain funny!!
> *Young Frankenstein—* absurdity, absurdity, absurdity. Great fun! Great parody. I love the ability to have fun with something quite serious.
>
> It's interesting to me that out of 5 films, 3 are comedies. Why? I love humor & irony. This is a real big part of my personality. I can take almost anything & find humor in it. For example, my first car accident.

Even these brief jottings reveal a great deal about each writer. What can we infer about the persons who wrote these responses?

For sample response 1:

➤ A sense of humor
➤ Wide variety of interests
➤ Awareness of details
➤ Extracts a serious thought from a seemingly insignificant event
➤ Has ability to draw inferences from specifics

For sample response 2:

➤ Wide range of tastes in movies
➤ Person who likes humor
➤ Person who likes absurdity
➤ An analytical thinker
➤ Self-aware thinker
➤ A person who can distill the topic and have it trigger something new: from commonality in diverse subjects, such as movies to a car accident

Sample 3: I'm outraged by: hunger in America

America: land of plenty—a chicken in every pot. Maybe—but what about those who don't even have a pot?

OUTRAGE RE: HUNGER IN AMERICA

WASTE	SOLUTIONS?
Extreme—freegans—only eat what restaurants throw away	INN—Interfaith Nutrition Network
Restaurant buffets	Rock stars—written in contracts that all leftover food collected by volunteers & given to soup kitchens
Look at my own trash cans	Food drive—collect free turkeys from supermarkets
	Volunteer at food kitchen—Thanksgiving for all!

Sample 4: I took a chance: Telling my friends that we have to stop making fun of a teacher

Scene: My HS library. Junior year: I'm sitting with my friends around a library table doing homework. Mrs. Crenshaw, the old librarian, enters and begins to play the piano in the front of the library.

Situation: Crenshaw begins to play, fumbles, tries again, fumbles as she tries to play a classical piece. She always began this way, and it took several minutes for her to begin to play well. This one evening, all of my friends and myself began to laugh and giggle loudly as we made fun of "Old Crank" and imitated her gnarled fingers hitting the keys. Had to go to the front of the library for something and passed her. She was crying.

<table>
<tr><td>Dilemma:</td><td>Did she hear us laughing? Was she crying because of her arthritic hands? Was she sorry she couldn't play the way she used to? Was she crying for her lost youth? All I knew was that she was crying, and I believed it was because of us. Felt bad. What should I do?</td></tr>
<tr><td>Resolution:</td><td>Went back to my group & told them about what I saw & talked about how we hurt her & how we needed to change our behavior and attitude. Made friends with Mrs. Crenshaw. Heard lots of stories. Laughed a lot with her. Felt better about being kind to people rather than making fun of those who are different.</td></tr>
</table>

What can we infer about sample responses 3 and 4?

For sample response 3:

➤ Writer has genuine humanitarian concerns.
➤ Has obviously thought about topic: factual, informative, varied solutions.
➤ Can easily impose structure on a subject.
➤ Can see solutions to a problem.
➤ Has a sense of commitment.

For sample response 4:

➤ Writer is compassionate.
➤ Is observant.
➤ Knows how to draw from memory.
➤ Self-reflective.
➤ Honest about shortcomings.
➤ Narrative leads to an insight.
➤ Reveals more about self than about Mrs. Crenshaw.

Sample 5: Favorite painting

Degas' Ballerina oil/copy
Hangs in living room

Left—series of curtains   Middle—on one leg is star ballerina
ballerinas tucked inside   balanced ridiculously
                                    dress so low, but no cleavage—why?
                                        little blotch of flowers

Hovers—precariously & powerfully
awkward & graceful

Tenuous position like most of my life—searching for balance—not sure

Center stage—worried what those in the wings think
Striving for beauty

What can we infer about this writer?

➤ Observant of details
➤ Asks questions
➤ Understands composition
➤ Responds to impressionism
➤ Uses art to examine self
➤ Reveals personal doubts and goals

Sample 6: A challenge met

Learning how to throw a decent basket from the foul line

On varsity basketball team. Unable to make a decent foul shot. Missed more often than I hit the basket. Thought it was a natural-born talent. Either you could or you couldn't. Always hated to be fouled. Made all kinds of excuses why I was lousy at foul shots.

Coach always said,

> "Practice. Practice your arm work, your hand-eye coordination, your knee bends."

> "Practice lifting your body with the ball."

> "You need more practice."

>> I did practice—but only about 5 minutes out of basketball practice. No real improvement. Told to practice more. I resisted. Finally, I couldn't stand my own failures. Started practicing foul shots 15–20 minutes extra after each team practice. % went way up! Went from 30% to more than 70%.

> Practice does make perfect—well, almost.

What can we infer about the writer of sample 6?

➤ Has an interest in sports
➤ Desire to improve
➤ Willing to examine shortcomings
➤ Not a quitter
➤ Has pride in achievement

Get the gist of this exercise? Try several topics now, and you'll see that you DO have a wealth of experiences, interactions, quirks, and insights that make you an interesting individual —one the admissions people would like to know more about. Follow the models you've already examined.

☞ YOUR TURN ☜

You've probably been thinking about possible topics as you read through the previous sections of this chapter. Now it's your turn to do some *real* brainstorming in written form.

THE PROCESS

☑ Choose a topic from the list in the section "Your Very Own Personal Interview."

☑ Take five minutes and jot down everything that enters your mind about the particular topic.

☑ Take five more minutes and jot down everything you observe or infer about yourself in relation to what you've written and what it says about you.

☑ Try several of these. They may well become the foundation for your final essay—and you've had fun.

The following pages provide a format for completing the process.

TOPIC 1

The topic is:_____

My specific topic: _____

_____

_____

_____

_____

_____

5 minutes to jot down ideas _____

_____

_____

_____

_____

5 minutes to draw inferences about myself based on jottings

_____

_____

_____

_____

_____

_____

TOPIC 2

The topic is: _____

My specific topic: _____

_____

_____

_____

_____

_____

5 minutes to jot down ideas _____

_____

_____

_____

_____

_____

5 minutes to draw inferences about myself based on jottings

_____

_____

_____

_____

_____

_____

_____

_____

TOPIC 3

The topic is: _____

My specific topic: _____

_____

_____

_____

_____

_____

5 minutes to jot down ideas _____

_____

_____

_____

_____

_____

5 minutes to draw inferences about myself based on jottings

_____

_____

_____

_____

_____

_____

_____

Using the Materials You've Discovered

This is the skill we want you to develop and refine.

After you have spent serious time with the personal interview, it's time to prewrite your essay. Now you have to choose an episode or belief or activity that is critical to who you are. For example, let's assume that dance is your passion.

Using *dance* as your frame of reference, and with a few specific questions in mind, you **work the material.**

1. List several broad contexts to consider, such as a challenge, a triumph, a fear, a hope.

2. Decide on your topic, or passion, or episode. (We've chosen dance.) Prepare yourself thoroughly with all aspects of your choice: your actions, reactions, sights, people, sounds, places, emotions, etc.

3. Mold the information to fit the question. For example, using *dance* as your topic,

   ➤ An *academic lesson* might evolve from a choreographer's direction.

   ➤ You might discuss a *social challenge* in terms of an audition.

   ➤ Your most *treasured recreational moments* might be when you are moving to the music.

   ➤ Your *ethical goal* might be to bring dance to underprivileged children.

   ➤ A *personal or spiritual triumph* might be a difficult sequence you've mastered.

   ➤ An injury might force you to examine your *occupational goals*.

We're sure you get the idea. You take the basic area you're going to write about and tweak and modify it until it suits your purposes. (Make certain you adapt your essay to the specific needs of each of the colleges to which you are applying.) In other words, you've looked at the big picture, and now you are going to focus the scene into a tight shot that will be intense, alive, and unique to you. And when you do this, the admissions readers will truly hear **your voice.**

CHOOSING YOUR TOPIC

You've awakened your memory in Chapter 2; you're free-associating and seeing the potential in your responses to topics. Now it's time to put this "stuff" to work in the context of a *real* question (we will also use the word *prompt*). This chapter will introduce you to the most common application questions/prompts you will encounter. It will also deconstruct several of these questions and provide suggestions for approaching the assigned task. We have indicated the specific college asking the questions, but, obviously, we could not list questions for all the schools you may be considering. Be aware that many, many, schools use the same questions or variations on the topics we examine. In fact, many schools use the *Common Application Form*, and we also cover these questions in this chapter.

Even if you are not planning to apply to one of the schools cited, it is very important to read all the questions because sometimes reading a prompt in a different format will trigger a response in you and start you on the path to planning your essay for the college of your choice. There's an added bonus: thinking about each of these topics will prepare those of you who choose to go on a personal interview at your college or with one of its representatives. These ideas are representative of what you may be asked. How terrific; you'll have all the right answers because you've been probing your experiences throughout the personal interview process.

A Sampling of Some Typical College Application Essay Questions

QUESTION:

Choose and discuss a quotation or personal motto that reflects your values and beliefs and tells us something about the kind of person you are.—**Cornell University**

The choice of quotation can determine the tone and style of your essay. If you already have a personal favorite, go for it. If not, here are some tips:

- ☑ Pick up a copy of *Bartlett's Familiar Quotations* and randomly skim through it.
- ☑ Go online to various quotation sites and plug in topics of interest to you.
- ☑ Reflect on your favorite songs and extract lines that have possibilities.
- ☑ Review the novels, plays, and poems you have studied for great lines or mottos.
- ☑ Think of family sayings and their implications.

Remember, the idea is not only about choosing a quotation with potential, but also about communicating what that quotation reveals about your values and you as a person. Always give credit to the source of your choice, even if it is anonymous.

☞ YOUR TURN ☜

Tap into *your own* quotable memory.

FAVORITE   WHAT IT REVEALS ABOUT ME

Quotations: _____   _____

_____   _____

_____   _____

Lyrics: _____   _____

_____   _____

_____   _____

_____   _____

Mottos and aphorisms: _____   _____

_____   _____

_____   _____

_____   _____

QUESTION:

> *You have just completed your 300-page autobiography. Please submit page 217.*—**University of Pennsylvania**

This question allows you to reveal your future plans and aspirations. You must realize that the page number implies that you have lived a good portion of your life already. The voice you choose should reflect a level of maturity and reflection. You can utilize any or all of the rhetorical strategies and literary techniques to create your scenario and persona. Be creative. Use such techniques as dialogue, symbol, flashback, epiphany, mood, and tone to develop your essay. Remember, it must reveal you and your values.

☞ YOUR TURN ☜

Complete this activity with your imagination in high gear.

My age when I'm writing this autobiography is_____.

My age on page 217 will be _____.

Since page 300 is near the end of the book, my circumstances will be (be specific)

_____

_____

_____

_____

_____

My personal circumstances on page 217 will be (be specific) _____

_____

_____

_____

What this page (217) will reveal about me. _____

_____

_____

_____

_____

QUESTION:

Indicate a person who has had a significant influence on you and explain that influence.—**Harvard University**

Generally speaking, this question refers to real people with whom you have interacted. The pitfall of this question is that many students choose family members, which is perfectly fine, but it is often difficult to separate personal emotion from the point of the essay. By all means choose honestly, but remember that the admissions committee will be reading many, many, inspirational testaments to relatives. **Avoid being sentimental, and focus on the influence and its power in your life.**

QUESTION:

Describe a character in fiction, an historical figure, or a creative work (as in art, music, science, etc.) that has had an influence on you and explain that influence.—**Harvard University**

This question, similar to the one above, is easier for some students because it may not be as emotionally linked as the previous choice. Be honest. Do not choose a character that you think will impress the reader. Choose one that you truly respond to. (Remember how passionate Holden Caulfield was when he said he wanted to meet Eustacia Vye? He really let us in on his most private longings and value.)

Once again, **it is not just the character or work that you must address, but also the nature of the influence and its effect on you**.

☞ YOUR TURN ☜

Be honest when you do this next exercise.

MY MOST INFLUENTIAL PERSON (or character or work of art, etc.)

Who: _____

Why: _____

Influence: _____

_____

_____

_____

_____

Circumstance or episode I recall that illustrates this influence: _____

_____

_____

_____

_____

_____

_____

Its effect on me: _____

_____

_____

_____

_____

QUESTION:

Recall an occasion when you took a risk that you now know was the right thing to do.—**University of Pennsylvania**

This question requires that you reflect on the risk and explore the long-term effects of your decision. To construct a complete response, you must explain the nature of the risk, the reasons you took it, and how, with the benefit of time, you now know that you made the right decision. **It is always a plus if you can relate that decision to your current circumstances.**

☞ YOUR TURN ☜

Lower your application essay risk by completing the following chart:

The risk: _____

_____

_____

Why taken: _____

_____

_____

Specifics:_____

_____

_____

Right or not:_____

_____

_____

_____

_____

QUESTION:

What is your favorite word and why?—**University of Virginia**

A very challenging and creative question that is deceptive in its simplicity. Your choice will reveal your understanding of nuance and tone. It's a great question to have fun with—but don't jump to easy and trite responses. Think and explore the possibilities of language...and, of course, be yourself.

☞ YOUR TURN ☜

Sure, you have a word for it. Here's another memory-stretching exercise.

Word:_____

_____

Definitions(s): _____

_____

Why it's a favorite:_____

_____

_____

_____

QUESTION:

Have you witnessed a person who is close to you doing something you considered seriously wrong? Describe the circumstances, your thoughts, and how you chose to respond. If you discussed it with the person, was his/her justification valid? In retrospect, what, if anything, would you have done differently and why?—**Duke University**

Not for the faint-hearted, this question is very personal, and you need to consider all the requirements carefully. You must isolate a moral problem, share an intimate relationship, and analyze your situation and response. You may reveal more than you realize. Pay careful attention to your tone. Avoid pomposity and preaching. If applicable, remember to address the other person's rationale and its validity. And then you must include how time has or has not altered your view of the episode. An essay this complex is a rich opportunity if you are comfortable with it. If not, avoid it completely.

☞ YOUR TURN ☜

Here's your chance to play judge and jury.

The offense: _____ Your circumstances:_____

_____ _____

Who: _____ Your thoughts:_____

_____ _____

What:_____ Your response: _____

_____ _____

Where: _____	Your reflections over time: _____
_____	_____
Why: _____	Your rationale: _____
_____	_____
_____	The other's rationale: _____
_____	_____
_____	_____
_____	_____
_____	_____

The following questions are for *you* to examine and think about. Follow the form of the previous examples. These should give you a clear idea of the scope and variety of writing opportunities available to you. Give yourself permission to explore; talk about the questions; practice your jotting and inference skills. This is your application training, and it will pay off. The more familiar you are with the process, the less nervous you'll be, and the more confident you'll become.

AMHERST COLLEGE QUESTION

Please respond to one of the following quotations. We are eager to know more about you as a person. We hope to find out who you are, how you think, what you think about and how you choose to express yourself.

1. *"We seek [community] more often than we find it; we find it in odd and surprising ways; it is real but is also fragile, uncertain, and sometimes ambiguous."*—Amherst College, President Tom Gerety, Commencement Address, 1994

2. *"There is no use in trying,"* said Alice; *"one can't believe impossible things."* *"I dare say you haven't much practice,"* said the Queen. *"When I was your age, I always did it for half an hour a day. Why, sometimes I believed six impossible things before breakfast."*—Lewis Carroll, *Alice's Adventures in Wonderland*

UNIVERSITY OF VIRGINIA QUESTIONS

Look out any window in your home. What would you change and why?

What form of discrimination most concerns you?

Technophobe or technophile?

MASSACHUSETTS INSTITUTE OF TECHNOLOGY QUESTIONS

Life brings many disappointments as well as satisfactions. Could you tell us about a time in your life when you experienced disappointment, or faced difficult or trying circumstances?

Make up a question that is personally relevant to you, state it clearly and answer it. Feel free to use your imagination, recognizing that those who read it will not mind being entertained.

DUKE UNIVERSITY QUESTION

What has been your most profound or surprising intellectual experience?

UNIVERSITY OF CHICAGO QUESTION

What would you do with a superhuge jar of mustard?

CORNELL UNIVERSITY QUESTION

Tell us about an opinion you have had to defend. How has this affected your belief system?

EMORY UNIVERSITY QUESTION

Of the activities in which you have been involved, which has meant the most to you, and why?

JOHNS HOPKINS UNIVERSITY QUESTION

Please respond to the following, using whatever space and medium you like. If you had only 10 dollars, or the equivalent in another currency, to plan a day's adventure, where would you go, what would you do, and whom would you take with you?

PRINCETON UNIVERSITY QUESTIONS

If you were given one year to spend in service on behalf of others, what would you choose to do, and why?

What is the most difficult decision you've had to make? How did you go about making it?

What idea, invention, discovery or creation do you think has had the biggest impact on your life so far?

What is the most difficult decision you've had to make? How did you go about making it?

What particular accomplishment up to this point in your life has given you the greatest satisfaction? Briefly explain.

COLUMBIA UNIVERSITY QUESTION

Write an essay that conveys to the reader a sense of who you are. Possible topics include, but are not limited to, experiences which have shaped your life, the circumstances of your upbringing, your most meaningful intellectual achievement, the way you see the world—the people in it, events great and small, everyday life—or any personal theme which appeals to your imagination. Please remember that we are concerned not only with the substance of your prose but with your writing style as well.

YALE UNIVERSITY QUESTION

We ask you to write a personal essay that will help us to know you better. In the past, candidates have written about their families, intellectual and extracurricular interests, ethnicity or culture, school and community events to which they have had strong reactions, people who have influenced them, significant experiences, personal aspirations, or topics that spring entirely from their imaginations. You should feel confident that in writing about what matters to you, you are bound to convey a strong sense of who you are.

NORTHWESTERN UNIVERSITY QUESTION

What have you undertaken or done on your own in the last year or two that has nothing to do with academic work?

SWARTHMORE COLLEGE QUESTION

Imagine that you have the opportunity to travel back through time. At what point in history would you like to stop and why?

SIMMONS COLLEGE QUESTION

If you were to look back on your high school years, what advice would you give to someone beginning their high school career?

NEW YORK UNIVERSITY QUESTION

It has been said [by Andy Warhol] that "in the future everyone will be famous for fifteen minutes." Describe your fifteen minutes.

STANFORD UNIVERSITY QUESTIONS

What single adjective do you think would be most frequently used to describe you by those who know you best? Briefly explain.

We are often misled by the appearance of things, of people, even of ourselves. Write about an appearance that deceived you and analyze its significance to you.

The Long and Short of It

So far we've been trying to loosen you up, to open your mind to the vast resources you have at hand to write the personal statement that each college will demand of you. In addition, the college may want you to write responses to some short questions. In this situation, you may want to use the information you've previously mined to respond to the brief essay questions. The expectation is that these answers will be informative and concrete. Let's take a look at some of the questions drawn from a pool of colleges, plus the common application.

➤ Why did you choose _____ (college)?

➤ What do you hope to get from _____ (college)?

➤ What will you bring to _____ (college)?

➤ What field of study do you wish to pursue? Why?

➤ What extracurricular activity has been most meaningful to you and why?

➤ What work experience has been most meaningful to you and why?

➤ What personal activities have been most meaningful to you and why?

➤ Explain why a grade below B is not an accurate reflection of your academic ability.

➤ Explain why a particular part of your transcript is not an accurate reflection of your personal traits or your potential.

➤ Tell us what you did last Sunday (or the Sunday before that).

➤ What interests you most about your intended discipline?

➤ What led you to choose your intended field of study?

➤ What makes you feel that this college is a good match for you?

➡ **See Chapter 5 for some examples of short answer responses.**

WRITING THE ESSAY

It's time to get to the nitty-gritty of writing the essay. Before going any further, allow us to remind you that the application essay is not meant to serve as an English class essay with all of the expectations of analysis and argumentation finely honed to address a literary prompt. It is an essay in which you are introducing yourself to real people who are looking for a reason to invite you to their campus. And they understand that not every one of you is going to be an English major. **But it is important to be literate and engaging—in other words, an effective communicator. We're talking about purpose, choice, and voice.**

Spend a few minutes reviewing the following points with us.

First and foremost, BE YOURSELF. The college admissions officers want to get to know a real person, someone they would like to meet and talk with. It is this genuine character who has to catch their attention. If you are whimsical, be playful; if you are academic, be scholarly; if you are forthright, be direct. There is no single approach to success.

➡ **Remember that first impressions DO count.**

Choosing the Best Subject for You

Where do you begin? With the question—the question that is NOT going to ask you to analyze a Shakespearean sonnet, nor prove a math theorem, nor discuss the causes of the Civil War. The question IS going to provide the opportunity for a wide range of responses and approaches to topics designed to hit those areas not covered in other areas of the application process.

> **NOTE: Do NOT use your personal essay to restate information you've already provided in other sections of your application. Your grades, awards, extracurricular activities, employment, etc., have all been previously listed.** *Avoid redundancy.*

We're going to illustrate this process of choosing the right question for you by using the Common Application's list of personal statement prompts. Read each of the prompts carefully with an open mind. In all probability you will gravitate toward two or three of these topics. For the time being ignore the others.

Choose one of the following:

1. Evaluate a significant experience, achievement, risk you have taken, or ethical dilemma you have faced and its impact on you.

2. Discuss some issue of personal, local, national, or international concern and its importance to you.

3. Indicate a person who has had a significant influence on you, and describe that influence.

4. Describe a character in fiction, a historical figure, or a creative work (as in art, music, science, etc.) that has had an influence on you, and explain that influence.

5. A range of academic interests, personal perspectives, and life experiences adds much to the educational mix. Given your personal background, describe an experience that illustrates what you would bring to the diversity in a college community, or tell about an encounter that demonstrated the importance of diversity to you.

6. Topic of your choice.

A NOTE ABOUT CHOICE 6: By this time, if you have played with the brainstorming activities related to the personal interview section of this book, you may be ready to choose a topic that reflects your own passion and style. So be decisive and choose number 6, and move on to the next section of this chapter.

Many students are not comfortable with a blank canvas and might feel intimidated by the pure, open-ended nature of choice 6. If this describes you, ignore choice 6 and stay with us for the following section.

THE PROCESS

1. Read the topics again. Notice that each of the questions contains the word *you* or *your*. This is a very important part of the prompt. They want to hear *your* voice, *your* ideas, *your* values.

2. Quickly check the two or three that stand out, intrigue you, or grab your interest.

3. Deconstruct each of these choices as we did in Chapter 3 so that you understand what is required.

4. Return to your brainstorming notes from the personal interview section in Chapter 2 and look for the potential they may hold for a response to any of the two or three topics you've checked.

5. Keep an open mind. Allow for expanding boundaries and a willingness to supplement or delete ideas and materials.

6. Either use something you find in your brainstorming notes, or start the brainstorming process anew with the topics that interest you in mind.

7. Remember five minutes is all you should be spending on choosing your topic. If you are agonizing over a topic choice, it may be an indication that the topic is not suited to you and you should move on to another prompt.

WORKING WITH OUR TWO WRITERS

Our student writer Elvira has reread the Common Application topics, and prompts 5 and 6 interest her very much. She reviewed her personal interview (Chapter 2) and noticed that the following might provide material she could use to respond to those two essay topics (an experience that illustrates what you would bring to the diversity in a college community; topic of your choice).

A unique talent I have:	*playing alphabet categories*
I'm so frustrated by:	*this whole sleeping process!*
Don't ask me to...	*go to bed early*
Just once I'd like to:	*fall asleep quickly*

Each of these notes pointed to material that could be used to develop either topic 5 or 6. Elvira decided to write about her very real problem with insomnia. Because it's such an idiosyncratic topic, she chooses to work with prompt 6, which will give her more freedom to approach her subject: *Topic of your choice.*

Jake has reread the Common Application topics, and two of them have grabbed his interest: topics 1 and 3. Following the same process as Elvira did, Jake noticed certain material from his personal interview he could use to respond to those two prompts (a significant experience, risk, dilemma, etc., or an influential person).

The best of times:	**winning the championship**
The best thing I ever learned:	**to respect differences √**
I'm a survivor:	**of Coach Bender's practices**
I'm proudest of:	**making Mrs. Crenshaw smile √**
A challenge I met:	**learning to make good foul shots**
I took a chance:	**telling my friends that we have to stop making fun of a teacher √**
Sports and me—what a team:	**basketball**
An opinion I changed and why:	**old folks don't really interest me √**

Each of these notes pointed to material that could be related to either topic 1 or 3. One of his brainstorming jottings focused on a personal risk regarding a school librarian, and another told of being helped by his basketball coach to improve his foul shots. Jake feels comfortable with both topics, but he decides the "librarian and risk" is the better choice for his college. Therefore, he chooses to respond to topic 1: *Evaluate a significant experience, achievement, risk you have taken, or ethical dilemma you have faced and its impact on you.*

☞ YOUR TURN ☜

Review the list of prompts given in the first part of this chapter, and make a decision.

1. The topic(s) that interest me are ___1 ___2 ___3 ___4 ___5 ___6.

2. The specific items in my personal interview that seem to fit these topics are_____

_____

_____

_____

_____

3. After reviewing both the topics and my personal interview items, I've decided that the best choice of topics for me is_____

_____

_____

_____

_____

_____

After carefully reviewing her brainstorming notes and choosing her topic, Elvira needs to make two very important choices. The first concerns her strategy for presenting her ideas. She can choose from among exposition, cause-effect, narration, argument, etc. Her second choice will be the tone she wishes to establish for her essay. Will she be formal or informal, objective or personal, serious or humorous, sarcastic or reverent, etc.? Elvira's choices are:

Strategy: Exposition with literary references
Tone: Humorous and personal

She quickly writes a few notes about how she will organize her presentation.

Introduction: Quotation from *Hamlet* and *Macbeth*. ID the problem.

The body: Ways I fight insomnia:
　　　　　　T.V.
　　　　　　Reading
　　　　　　Games: A to Z
　　　　Benefits:
　　　　　　Crossword puzzles
　　　　　　Jeopardy
　　　　　　Conversation

Conclusion: "Life is what happens when you can't sleep." (Fran Liebowitz)
　　　　College = life
　　　　A to Z in college life

Jake also takes a careful look at his brainstorming notes and makes some decisions about how he will approach his topic.

> *Strategy:* Narrative in chronological order
> *Tone:* Serious and personal

He then jots down a few quick notes about how he will organize his essay:

Introduction: Set up scene in library.

The story: Mrs. Crenshaw playing piano.

My friends and I laugh at her poor playing and poke fun at her physical appearance and abilities.

I have to get something in front of room and must pass librarian at the piano.

I see Mrs. Crenshaw crying. <u>I think of my grandmother.</u>

I felt bad because I thought we had made her cry.

I go back to my group and tell them about this and ask them to stop and to make it up to her.

I was afraid, at first, that my friends would laugh at me or just plain reject my idea and I'd lose their respect.

They reluctantly agreed.

We made friends with the librarian. She told us stories, and we laughed a lot with her.

She smiled when she saw us. We became her student "guardians."

Result of risk: I learned the value of standing up for my principles, and I learned that older people have a lot to offer to young people like me.

☞ YOUR TURN ☜

Carefully consider how you would like to present your ideas to the admissions people.

Strategy: have decided to use the following primary strategy for my essay:

_____	Exemplification	_____	Contrast/comparison
_____	Cause-effect	_____	Description
_____	Definition	_____	Narration
_____	Other (identify) _____		

Tone: I would like the tone of my essay to be (check those that apply):

_____	Formal	_____	Whimsical	_____	Inspiring
_____	Informal	_____	Ironic	_____	Satiric
_____	Serious	_____	Nostalgic	_____	Argumentative
_____	Humorous	_____	Reflective		
_____	Critical	_____	Joyous		
_____	Sad	_____	Intellectual		
_____	Other (identify) _____				

Your own brief organizing notes:

_____

_____

_____

_____

_____

_____

_____

_____

The First Draft

Once the idea for your essay is fixed in your mind, it's time to begin to write the first draft.

Remember to:

- ☑ Choose a strategy and a tone.
- ☑ Write with a focus and a clear voice.
- ☑ Pay attention to clarity of thought, organization, and syntax.
- ☑ Engage the reader.
- ☑ Illuminate your idea with details, examples, anecdotes.
- ☑ Watch for tense consistency.
- ☑ Use active voice.
- ☑ Avoid sounding like a thesaurus. **Nothing is more awkward or turns readers off more than the use of pompous and inappropriate words. Be natural in your writing.** Imagine you are having a conversation with the reader.
- ☑ Keep it within the assigned word count.
- ☑ Check to see that you have addressed ALL of the requirements of the prompt (Chapter 3).

In the Beginning: Writing the Opening

Make the opening of your essay reach out and grab the reader. After all, your voice has to be heard above all the others yet to be read. **Bear in mind that the purpose of the opening is to begin to identify you as a unique individual and to introduce the topic and the tone of the essay.** The well-worn advice of your many English instructors works very well here.

Try to begin your essay with one of these:

- ☑ A real quotation you like
- ☑ A piece of dialogue

☑ A rhetorical question

☑ A startling statement

☑ An engaging anecdote

☑ A challenge

☑ A revelation

☑ An interesting fact

Because a blank page is often intimidating, we highly recommend that you try two or three different openings to get your writing mind in gear and to start those juices flowing. The body of your essay will develop from your opening. So don't be afraid to spend time on this first section of your essay.

Your opening may also be explicit or implicit. **An explicit response would make direct reference to the words of the prompt.** For example: *Repelling off the face of Mount Washington was the most challenging risk I've ever taken.* **An implicit opening presents a situation that illustrates the prompt without actually using its exact wording.** For example: *My heart pounded, my hands were sweaty, and my throat was so dry I didn't know if I was going to be able to face the director and give my soliloquy when I tried out for the lead in* Grease.

🎓 WORKING WITH OUR TWO WRITERS 🐵

Let's consider Elvira's drafts of the opening for her essay.

1. *(Dialogue)* "Did I wake you, Sleeping Beauty?" It was another wisecracking friend on the phone Saturday morning at 11:30. "Big deal, so I'm still sleeping at noon on the weekends," I muttered under my breath. Don't they know that the last time I got a good night's sleep was last Tuesday? I haven't slept five hours in a row since I was three. I am an insomniac—and proud of it!

2. *(Interesting details)* Arapaho, Blackfoot, Cherokee, Dakota, Erie…Lenape, Mohican, Nez Perce… Will I ever fall asleep before I reach the Utes and Zunis? I, too, am a member of a unique tribe. I am an insomniac.

3. *(Startling statement)* My name is Elvira, and I'm an insomniac. I carry my curse everywhere—I cannot hide. It betrays me with a stifled yawn in the middle of a conversation, a half-lidded gaze that never quite sees its subject, and a nodding head that jerks awake at inopportune moments. My classmates' laughter mocks me in math class when my chin rests on my chest, finally at ease. My mouth falls open and gentle bubbling sounds escape my lips. Where is my respite? My slumber? My lullaby and good night?

4. *(Quotation)* "To sleep, perchance to dream. Ay there's the rub." Well, move over, Hamlet, because I can't wait to sleep. I feel more like Macbeth who "murdered sleep" than someone who's worried about a few bad dreams. In fact, I calculate that I haven't slept for at least ten of my seventeen years.

Elvira decided on opening 4 because she can incorporate the other details into the essay under this umbrella introduction.

Let's take a look at Jake's three drafts of the opening for his essay.

1. *(Quotation)* A couple of weeks ago my AP Government teacher put a quotation on the board that really got to me. It sounds really simple, but the more I thought about it while our class discussed what it meant, the more it meant to me. "What you risk reveals what you value" (Jeannette Winterson). Everybody was talking about politics, business, and sports, but I was thinking about something that happened between my friends and me and a teacher last year.

2. *(Dialogue)* "Wanna bet how long it takes for 'Old Crank' to get going today?" I said this to my friends as we watched Mrs. Crenshaw make her limpy way to the piano that was in the front of the library. My friends and I had set up our "study hall" in the back of the library, and every so often we would be there when our old, feeble librarian would wander up to the piano. We figured she was hard of hearing and really was unaware that we were even there. Mrs. Crenshaw always seemed to be in her own world and definitely not a part of ours.

3. *(Statement)* Most people remember events that have a great influence upon them. Well, I have one that involves something that happened between my friends and me and a teacher last year.

After considering each of the openings, Jake immediately rejects his third draft because it is just too simplistic and immature. He chooses to open his essay with the quotation because he sees that he can easily incorporate the dialogue opening into the actual story.

☞ YOUR TURN ☜

You've got to start somewhere, so here's the starting line. Give yourself the chance to write two or three different types of openings for your essay. Carefully review ALL of your personal notes and brainstorming up to this point.

Opening 1 (Type:) _____

_____

_____

_____

_____

_____

_____

_____

_____

Opening 2 (Type:) _____

_____

_____

_____

_____

_____

_____

_____

_____

_____

_____

Opening 3 (Type:)_____

_____

_____

_____

_____

_____

_____

_____

After considering each of my openings, I've decided on _____ 1 _____ 2 _____ 3

because _____

_____

_____

_____

Writing the Body of the Essay

The body of your essay will elaborate on the situation established in your opening or introduction. In addition to addressing the prompt, it must present a sense of who the writer is. To accomplish this, you will need to make choices about:

Particular strategies: Cause-effect, contrast-comparison, definition, description, exemplification, narration, etc.

Organization: Chronological order, most-to-least important point, least-to-most important point, specific to general, general to specific, etc.

Details: What subtext about you is revealed by your choice of specifics?

Diction: What does your choice of words reveal about you?

Syntax: What does your sentence structure tell the reader about your command of the English language?

Connective tissue: Those words and phrases that link each of your points to both your opening and the prompt.

➡ **Remember, whatever you choose to write about,
your ultimate goal is to present yourself as worthy of consideration
for admission to this particular college or university.**

 **WORKING WITH OUR TWO WRITERS**

Elvira has reconsidered all of her presentation choices, and she has reviewed her organization notes. Now she is ready to write the body of her essay.

The Body of Elvira's Essay

Now don't get me wrong—I'm not complaining. Actually, my life is really more interesting because of my affliction. I bet you don't know that yak tail can be made into a soup *and* a dessert. *Iron Chef* taught me that one morning at 3 a.m. In fact, I've taken rides on antique railroad cars across Europe, surfed off Patagonia, and redecorated my bedroom in the style of California kitsch for under

$100. And all of this happened after midnight! From *Friends* to *Frasier* to the Food Network, I struggle every night to T.V. or not to T.V.

But I always need a backup plan. (After all I've seen the *Friends* episode where Phoebe gives birth at least 12 times.) So I read. My favorites are mysteries—-not really a good idea because they get me so nervous I have to keep reading. *Some nights I finish an entire Stephen King novel even though I risk falling asleep during study hall or lunch with my head on my chest, my mouth open, little bubbles escaping my lips. At least I'm improving my literacy skills.*

Actually, insomnia forces me to be more creative. One of my favorite sleep inducers is a game of alphabetical categories. I pick a topic, start at the beginning, and fill in the appropriate responses. Shades of blue: aqua, baby, cerulean, Delft; leafy vegetables: arugula, beet greens, chicory, dandelion; three-syllable girls' names: Annabel, Bethany, Christina, Daffodil (okay, so I cheat once in a while). And my personal favorite, Native American tribes: Arapaho, Blackfoot, Cree, Dakota, Erie, right down to Ute and Zuni.

The best part of not sleeping is that I'm a whiz at crosswords and *Jeopardy*. Plus I can hold a conversation with anyone about pioneer life, weather disasters, or Mafia burial grounds. And I know how to artificially inseminate koala bears, but that's a story for another night.

Jake has followed the same process as Elvira and writes the following:

The Body of Jake's Essay

As we usually did, my friends and I had set up our "study hall" in the library of our school. We liked it there because we were left alone for the most part in the back of the room. You should know that there was a large piano in the front of the library. I don't know why, but it's been there ever since I've been a student here. After school, people sometimes would go in there and play around on it. One of these people was the librarian, Mrs. Crenshaw, who we thought was at least a hundred years old. I guess she even played during school because we heard her playing a lot during the day when no one was in there, or she thought no one was in there.

This one day, Mrs. Crenshaw made her limpy way to the piano. She probably didn't know we were in the back, or she couldn't see or hear us with her ancient eyes and ears.

"Wanna bet how long it takes for 'Old Crank' to get going today?" I said to my gang as we watched her inch her way on to the seat and lift open the piano cover.

As usual, Mrs. Crenshaw began to fumble and stumble along the keyboard as she tried to play a classical piece of music. And, as usual, we all laughed and punched each other as we made fun of her attempts to get her gnarled fingers to hit the right keys.

For some reason, I needed to use the dictionaries in the front of the library near the piano. I went up to the front and passed by the piano and 'Old Crank.'

She was crying.

I don't know why, but I thought of my grandmother just then and what I would think if I saw her crying.

Did Mrs. Crenshaw hear us laughing? Was she crying because her hands hurt from arthritis? Was she sorry she couldn't play the way she used to? Was she crying because she was old?

All I knew was that she was crying, and I believed it was because of us, and I felt really bad and guilty. I kept thinking about what I'd feel like and what I'd do if Mrs. Crenshaw were my grandmother. I knew I had to go back to my table of friends and tell them what I saw and felt and what I thought we should do. At first I was afraid that they would just plain reject my idea and laugh at me, and I'd end up losing their respect. But I never knew how much influence I had with them, because when I told them about Mrs. Crenshaw crying and that I wanted us to stop and to make it up to 'Old Crank,' they said okay. Maybe they thought of their grandmothers, too.

We all made our way up to the piano. Mrs. Crenshaw looked up, and it was like she saw us for the first time. We introduced ourselves, even though we knew she knew who we were. We asked her about the music and her piano playing. We began to be her student "guardians." Over the rest of the school year, she told us many stories, and we laughed a lot with her.

Mrs. Crenshaw became our "school grandmother."

☞ YOUR TURN ☜

Following the process used by both Elvira and Jake, it's now time for you to write the first draft of the body of your essay. Remember, this part of your essay is an elaboration of what you introduced in your opening.

The body of your essay: _____

_____

_____

_____

_____

_____

_____

_____

_____

_____

_____

_____

_____

_____

_____

_____

_____

Writing the Conclusion

A conclusion does not have to be a summary or restatement of the main idea of what you have just written. Your essay is a brief presentation, not a 500-page doctoral dissertation. The reader can remember your few words of introduction.

Here, as in your opening or introduction, you can choose to be either explicit or implicit. An explicit ending might state:

> *Tim, our mailman, was an unlikely role model for most of my neighborhood, but to me, he was a superhero. I learned to find greatness in unexpected places.*

If the writer wanted to use an implicit approach, he could write:

> *Since that awful year I spent in my prison of a cast, I know it wasn't the exotic stamps, nor the mail order catalogs, nor the magazines; it was Tim who made all the difference.*

You can use this portion of your essay to:

- ☑ Make a final dramatic point.
- ☑ Reveal an insight gained from the ideas presented in the body of your essay.
- ☑ Connect you to the college.
- ☑ Leave the reader with a provocative, final point about you.
- ☑ Create an open-ended invitation to get to know you better.

 WORKING WITH OUR TWO WRITERS

Elvira has decided to end her essay with a quotation that both refers to the opening and makes a connection between her and the college, plus a provocative statement about herself. Here is her ending:

Fran Liebowitz said, "Life is what happens when you can't sleep." The way I figure it, I probably won't get much sleep for the next four years. I can't bear the thought of missing a single moment of life at college. I'm looking forward to taking courses from astronomy to zoology, of studying art and zygotes, of meeting Alpha Beta Gammas and Zeta Tau Epsilons. After all, there will always be time to sleep tomorrow and tomorrow and tomorrow.

Jake, on the other hand, chooses to present an insight he gained from the experience he narrated in the body of his essay. Here is what he wrote:

I took a risk, but I learned the value of standing up for my principles, and I learned that older people have much to offer to young people like me. And I made a new friend.

Notice that Elvira's and Jake's endings are NOT summaries of their essays but rather final remarks the writers felt added something positive to their presentations, something that can help the admissions people know more about each of them.

☞ YOUR TURN ☜

Now that you've written the first draft of the body of your essay, you need to think about how you will end your presentation. Just what is it you want to leave the readers thinking about when they finish your essay?

I've decided to use the following method(s) to close my application essay:

_____ Leave the reader with a provocative, final point.

_____ Reveal an insight gained from the ideas presented in the body of my essay.

_____ Connect myself to the college.

_____ Create an open-ended invitation to get to know me better.

The first draft of my ending (Type:_____)

_____

_____

_____

_____

_____

_____

_____

_____

_____

_____

_____

_____

_____

Reading between the Lines

Keep in mind that the application essay is your introduction to your college. **It creates an initial impression just as you create one when you personally meet someone for the first time.**

When you receive a college brochure or go online to the Web site of a college you're interested in, what is it that first impresses you? Words or images? Be honest. We're betting that the vast majority of you will respond with "images." Why? This is what grabs your attention. It's what allows you to get a feel for the place. And you probably have an emotional response to the setting, to the faces, to the overall ambiance. It's visceral; you can't help it. It's your initial impression.

So, too, is your college application essay going to result in an initial impression—an image of you that only you can create.

➡ **Your words will form the reader's initial impression of you.**

The reader "reads" between the lines and forms a very definite opinion about you and about whether or not you will be a good fit for this college.

When you make your choices about which college or university you want to apply to, *you* are most likely thinking about:

- ➤ **Location** (north, south, east, west, urban, suburban, rural, foreign)
- ➤ **Campus** (large, small, modern, classical, traditional, institutional)
- ➤ **Population** (diversity, size, male-female ratio, class size, teacher-student ratio)
- ➤ **Courses** offered (major and minor subjects, degrees offered)
- ➤ **Reputation** (academics, faculty, sports, social life, connections)

On the other hand, the reader of your essay is most likely interested in:

- ➤ Enthusiasm
- ➤ Intelligence
- ➤ Uniqueness
- ➤ Scholarship
- ➤ Ability to communicate
- ➤ The fit for this college

➡ So you must understand that every choice you make in your essay has the potential to be interpreted by someone else.

Consider the following excerpts from different application essays.

> *Football is my life. I train twelve months of the year, not just during football season. During the off-season, I'm weight-training, conditioning, adhering to a strict diet, and practicing plays.*

The student who wrote this passage may have had as his personal interest the desire to show that football is his passion. However, the practiced reader could infer that the candidate:

- ➤ Is dedicated
- ➤ Shows the capability of long-term commitments
- ➤ Recognizes the link between hard work and success
- ➤ Has self-discipline

- ➤ Practices time management
- ➤ Prioritizes
- ➤ and on and on.

The reader recognizes that these attributes stand the writer in good stead for this college regardless of the topic he chooses to write about.

Now consider this next application essay excerpt.

> *The day I got my report card with a 92% on my math final was the best day of my junior year. I finally got back at Mr. Smith. All year long he had picked on me and took points off anything I handed in, even if I had a good excuse. Because of him, I stopped participating in class and hated math. I realized I could win by teaching myself to spite him, and I did.*

Although this writer intends to show how he overcame a difficult situation and triumphed, what should be a positive statement has presented instead a portrait of him in a negative light.

The student's successful grade aside, the reader of this excerpt reads between the lines and could infer that the student:

- ➤ Is immature
- ➤ Is stubborn
- ➤ Sees himself as a victim
- ➤ Easily places blame on others
- ➤ Looks for excuses
- ➤ Has a negative attitude

For the reader, this is not a likely candidate for consideration.

➡ Take the time to read between YOUR lines.

You can do this by placing yourself in the role of an admissions reader, or you could ask someone you trust to read between the lines and tell you what he or she can infer from what you've written.

🎓 WORKING WITH OUR TWO WRITERS 🤓

What can a reader infer after reading each of our writers' essays and reading between the lines?

Elvira's Essay

To sleep, perchance to dream. Ay, there's the rub." Well, move over, Hamlet, because I can't wait to sleep. I feel more like Macbeth who "murdered sleep" than someone who's worried about a few bad dreams. By my calculations, I haven't had a good night's sleep since 1997. I am an insomniac.

Now don't get me wrong—I'm not complaining. Actually, my life is really more interesting because of my affliction. I bet you don't know that yak tail can be made into a soup and a dessert. Iron Chef taught me that one morning at 3 a.m. In fact, I've taken rides on antique railroad cars across Europe, surfed off Patagonia, and redecorated my bedroom in the style of California kitsch for under $100. And all of this happened after midnight! From *Friends* to *Frasier* to the Food Network, I struggle every night to T.V. or not to T.V.

But I always need a backup plan. (After all I've seen the *Friends* episode where Phoebe gives birth at least 12 times.) So I read. My favorites are mysteries—not really a good idea because they get me so nervous I have to keep reading till it's light out. Some nights I finish an entire Stephen King novel even though I risk falling asleep during study hall or lunch with my head on my chest, my mouth open, little bubbles escaping my lips. At least I'm improving my literacy skills.

Actually, insomnia forces me to be more creative. One of my favorite sleep inducers is a game of alphabetical categories. I pick a topic, start at the beginning, and fill in the appropriate responses. Shades of blue: aqua, baby, cerulean, Delft; leafy vegetables: arugula, beet greens, chicory, dandelion; three-syllable girls' names: Annabel, Bethany, Christina, Daffodil (okay, so I cheat once in a while). And my personal favorite, Native American tribes: Arapaho, Blackfoot, Cree, Dakota, Erie, right down to Ute and Zuni.

The best part of not sleeping is that I'm a whiz at crosswords and *Jeopardy*. Plus I can hold a conversation with anyone about pioneer life, weather disasters, or Mafia burial grounds. And I know how to artificially inseminate koala bears, but that's a story for another night.

Fran Liebowitz said, "Life is what happens when you can't sleep." The way I figure it, I probably won't get much sleep for the next four years. I can't bear the thought of missing a single moment of life at college. I'm looking forward to taking courses from astronomy to zoology, of studying art and zygotes, of meeting Alpha Beta Gammas and Zeta Tau Epsilons. After all, there will always be time to sleep tomorrow and tomorrow and tomorrow.

If we *read between the lines*, what does this essay reveal about its writer? We can infer that she:

➤ Has a sense of humor
➤ Has a sense of irony
➤ Is well read
➤ Is introspective
➤ Is interested in a wide variety of subjects
➤ Is a go-getter
➤ Relates her circumstances to the upcoming college experience
➤ Deliberately imposes a structure

Jake's Essay

A couple of weeks ago my AP Government teacher put a quotation on the board that really got to me. It sounds really simple, but the more I thought about it while our class discussed what it meant, the more it meant to me. "What you risk reveals what you value" (Jeannette Winterson). Everybody was talking about politics, business, and sports, but I was thinking about something that happened between my friends and me and a teacher last year.

As we usually did, my friends and I had set up our study hall in the library of our school. We liked it there because we were left alone for the most part in the back of the room. You should know that there was a large piano in the front of the library. I don't know why, but it's been there ever since I've been a student here. After school, people sometimes would go in there and play around on it. One of these people was the librarian, Mrs. Crenshaw, who we thought was at least a hundred years old. I guess she even played during school because we heard her playing a lot during the day when no one was in there, or she thought no one was in there.

This one day, Mrs. Crenshaw made her pained way to the piano. She probably didn't know we were in the back, or she couldn't see or hear us with her ancient eyes and ears.

"Wanna bet how long it takes for 'Old Crank' to get going today?" I said to my gang as we watched her inch her way on to the seat and lift open the piano cover.

As usual, Mrs. Crenshaw began to fumble and stumble along the keyboard as she tried to play a classical piece of music. And, as usual, we all laughed and punched each other as we made fun of her attempts to get her gnarled fingers to hit the right keys.

For some reason, I needed to use the dictionaries in the front of the library near the piano. I went up to the front and passed by the piano and 'Old Crank.'

She was crying.

I don't know why, but I thought of my grandmother just then and what I would think if I saw her crying.

Did Mrs. Crenshaw hear us laughing? Was she crying because her hands hurt from arthritis? Was she sorry she couldn't play the way she used to? Was she crying because she was old?

All I knew was that she was crying, and I believed it was because of us, and I felt really bad and guilty. I kept thinking about what I'd feel like and what I'd do if Mrs. Crenshaw were my grandmother. I knew I had to go back to my table of friends and tell them what I saw and felt and what I thought we should do. At first I was afraid that they would just plain reject my idea and laugh at me, and I'd end up losing their respect. But I never knew how much influence I had with them, because when I told them about Mrs. Crenshaw crying and that I wanted us to stop and to make it up to 'Old Crank,' they said okay. Maybe they thought of their grandmothers, too.

We all made our way up to the piano. Mrs. Crenshaw looked up, and it was like she saw us for the first time. We introduced ourselves, even though we knew she knew who we were. We asked her about the music and her piano playing. We began to be her student "guardians." Over the rest of the school year, she told us many stories, and we laughed a lot with her.

Mrs. Crenshaw became our "school grandmother."

I took a risk, but I learned the value of standing up for my principles, and I learned that older people have much to offer to young people like me. And I made a new friend.

What does this essay reveal about its writer? We can infer that he is:

➤ Popular with a group of friends
➤ Sensitive
➤ Basically kind
➤ An individual who thinks for himself
➤ Probably close with his family
➤ A person with leadership qualities
➤ A person who reflects on his actions

☞ YOUR TURN ☜

Okay, either you or someone you trust must read your essay. After *reading between the lines,* list the characteristics and qualities that the reader can infer about you.

I can infer the following about the writer of this essay: _____

_____

_____

_____

_____

_____

_____

_____

_____

_____

_____

Responding to the Short-Answer Questions

Some colleges require not only a fully developed personal essay but also a series of questions requiring brief, direct responses. These questions are highly specific, and your objective is to provide particular, concrete information to supplement the other sections of your application. Typically, these questions include topics such as:

- ➤ *Tell us about your most significant extracurricular activity.*
- ➤ *Why do you want to attend this college?*
- ➤ *What will you bring to this campus?*
- ➤ *Tell us about a creative project.*
- ➤ *What was your most meaningful intellectual experience?*
- ➤ *Are there any mitigating or special circumstances you wish to convey that will provide additional information about a section of your application or about your personal situation?*

We know this goes without saying, but if you are required to answer questions like these, do not use the very same response with the same wording from your longer personal essay. We recommend that you go back to Chapter 2 and reread your personal interview, consider your brainstorming notes, and review the first draft of your personal essay. If there's any material that appears to be usable, by all means expand it.

Unlike the personal essay, the short-response section is looking for highly specific information about you. This is not the time to elaborate and philosophize. What you want to do is:

- ➤ Use your opening to immediately address the topic without actually repeating it.
- ➤ Provide specific details that refer only to the given topic.
- ➤ Consider each sentence to be capable of becoming a topic sentence in a longer essay.
- ➤ Be specific. Be clear. Be direct. Be brief.
- ➤ Avoid being redundant.

Read the following effective, short-response examples from students just like you.

STUDENT SAMPLES

This student responds to the question "Why have you chosen Emory?"

Emory fits. I saw strangers welcoming an unfamiliar face. I saw bright flowers, picturesque buildings, students jogging under the shade of the trees. I saw green everywhere. I took off my sweatshirt and enjoyed the day in summer clothing. I conversed with teachers, all eager to share their knowledge. I took a deep breath, looked around, and thought, "Emory fits."

I love to learn. I looked at the courses offered at Emory and felt a thrill of excitement as I imagined the possibilities, the subjects I have yet to explore. I have an interest in law, a profession I would like to investigate further. Because I do not have to choose my major until the end of my sophomore year, I will have the freedom to further discover my interests, to examine new subjects, and to determine my true passion. With the help of Emory, I will be able to reach my potential and make the most of my abilities. I want to explore capabilities and my aspirations with the assistance of my ideal university. Emory fits.

—Danielle Labadorf

COMMENTS: This response
> ➤ Has a strong introduction
> ➤ Indicates she's done some research on the university
> ➤ Is brief, direct, and positive
> ➤ Uses repetition to emphasize her main point and to create unity
> ➤ Emphasizes that she and Emory are a good match

This prompt asked for a response to the following: *Sharing intellectual interests is an important aspect of university life. Describe an experience or idea that you find intellectually exciting and explain why.*

Astronomy. The universe. Supernovae, galaxies, stars, quasars, fate. This topic is so fascinating that I can envision myself further exploring it in my lifetime. Last summer, I had the opportunity to learn about various aspects of this science, and ever since, I have fallen deeply in love with it.

One of the first lessons involved watching scientist Margaret Geller's video, "So Many Galaxies, So Little Time." I was immediately lured into the atmosphere of the telescopes at the team's observatory. Although the film was not one of obvious excitement, I became engrossed. While other students were amused with the creation of the video (after all, it was produced by scientists), I was immersed in the science it described. I imagined working at an observatory like that, or just viewing the stars through a high-tech telescope.

I often lay awake at night thinking of the mysteries in the universe that we have yet to discover. My heart leaps at such a reflection. I know that in my future I would like to continue my astronomical studies and hopefully have the chance to witness a natural phenomenon (such as a comet in action). I cannot think of a more incredibly thrilling experience.

—Grace Lin

COMMENTS: Direct and specific, this short response provides concrete information to address the prompt. Too often applicants write vague and general reactions. Use this as a model that captures the interest, explains the stimulus, and alludes to future study.

In response to the question "What is your favorite word, and why?" this student wrote:

A crisp, clean piece of paper. Breathing in the crisp, fall air. Biting into a crisp, red apple. Even the sound of the word sends a shudder through my body. Its gentle sound and the way it rolls off my tongue give it a flow, a rhythm. I do not remember when the fascination began, but I have always been drawn to the word "crisp." The dictionary defines it as "pleasingly firm and fresh, lively and sprightly, or bracing and invigorating." However, "crisp" holds a different meaning to me. It goes beyond a one word definition and into the depths of my emotions. It is the feeling of brisk efficiency I get when my field hockey stick makes contact with the ball in one, clean, crisp stroke. It is the feeling of drinking hot apple cider in the fall and walking over the crisp, crunching leaves. It is knowing that after my long, hard day of work, I will be paid with the crisp dollar bills I treasure in my pocket.

I am pleasingly firm in my opinions and fresh in the ideas I present to others. I am lively and sprightly, always ready for a challenge, a debate, or an unknown adventure. I am invigorated by sunshine, Phish, and chocolate-covered strawberries. Crisp. The way I think, feel, and act.

—Karin Hoesl

COMMENTS : In this reply, the reader can see:
- ➤ Three opening phrases that are brief, direct, and specific which are in themselves *crisp*
- ➤ Aspects of *crisp* illustrated in the first paragraph
- ➤ *Crisp* related to the writer's own personal experiences
- ➤ The conclusion constructed of a brief and direct pair of phrases that unify the entire response and connect to the opening

Consider how the following student responds to "Tell us about your most significant extracurricular activity."

What do you want to be when you grow up?" I remember this question plaguing me at the mere age of five, for I did not want to be a teacher or a veterinarian or an astronaut like every other student in my class. In fact, I had no clue, not even a hint, as to what my ideal profession would be. That is until I joined the mock trial team. From the very first meeting, I realized that this extracurricular activity was different from any other. I did not participate to kill time or to socialize; it was a club I joined because I found that I had a genuine interest in the law. Every day I attended the meetings with an open mind, eager to soak up any information I could get. In the courtroom, I found I was focused, on task, and determined. Once I joined the team, once I began working on different cases and learning more about the legal profession, a sudden fire ignited inside of me. I found my passion. Mock trial was not just an extracurricular activity at which I excelled; it was an activity that helped me realize my future goals and finally enabled me to answer that once unanswerable question.

—Danielle Labadorf

COMMENTS : The writer of this single paragraph:

- ➤ Draws the reader in with an introductory piece of dialogue
- ➤ Passionately enumerates the cause and effects of joining the mock trial team
- ➤ Constructs a final sentence that refers to the introduction

This short answer is in response to the question "What was your most meaningful intellectual experience?"

In my quest for knowledge, I found something beyond AP courses that sparked my interest. After taking courses at the Lab for numerous years, I wanted to investigate the evolving world of genetics. After reading various materials on genetics, I decided to combine both my love of horses and genetics into research that would have a significant impact on both the equine and medical communities. Currently conducting independent research at the Lab, I have learned two of the most important lessons of a scientist: patience and determination. Both of these qualities developed after spending hours upon hours at the Lab hoping and praying that my protocol would work. It was almost a year before I received my first equus mitochrondrial DNA sequence. This accomplishment was a reward well worth the time and commitment. And, this experience has opened the doors of learning to me.

—Ashley Peterson

COMMENTS : This student writer:

- ➤ Speaks on a very mature level about a topic that she obviously feels comfortable with
- ➤ Writes on an intellectual level and does not trivialize her experience or patronize her reader
- ➤ Uses a tone that is formal, serious, and objective throughout
- ➤ Connects her experience to her future academic success

This student writes in response to the question, "What do you hope to do once you leave college?"

The world that no one sees, the one that many choose not to see, is the one I desire to venture into. The dense jungle of cries and screams, the arid desert where life is barely able to be sustained, the city where swarms of the hopeless flock the streets; this is where my journey will take me. In times of heartache one looks toward another for relief and comfort. What will happen to those who have no one? To be a friend to the friendless and to aid those who have lost faith in the world, this is my desire.

—Saira Hussain

COMMENTS : This brief answer to the prompt:
- ➤ Clearly demonstrates the sincerity, fervor, and sensitivity of the writer
- ➤ Effectively describes a scene that has truly moved the writer
- ➤ Because of its brevity avoids being overly sentimental
- ➤ Summons up an exotic and unknown locale for the reader

This prompt asks the student to "Tell us something about yourself that is not reflected in the rest of your application."

I giggled as I passed a note to my best friend, Becky. She looked up at the teacher, scribbled some words down, and then passed it back. I opened it carefully, and smiled. "Ben was looking at you before," it read. "He surely likes you back." I grinned at Becky and snugly folded the note into my notebook. Drawn all over my papers in big loopy handwriting were the words, "I love Ben." Of course, it was normal adolescent infatuation.

Naturally, his heart was what I vied for in the next several months. One day after school, I thought back to that morning when he actually said hello and we smiled at each other. Upon my return home, I wanted to tell someone. I wanted to tell anyone, to just express my feelings in some kind of crazy manner.

Too lazy to find my diary, I ripped a page out of a spiral notebook carelessly and started scribbling words on it. Any words. All words. I wanted to explain the butterflies raging in my stomach. The longing I felt deep within my heart. The very first poem I ever wrote was simply created from a collection of words that pertained to my fierce emotions.

Gratefully, I wonder how it could be that something seemingly so innocent as a crush on a young boy in middle school could bring such a gift to my life. No, it wasn't Ben's heart; it was something so much more valuable to me. It was the love of words. My emotions coupled with my passion for language created poetry.

—Grace Lin

COMMENTS : There is a sweet and tender sense of memory in the essay that belies the underlying and surprise conclusion—the deep passion of the author for language and poetry. A seemingly universal and innocent awakening of love is the catalyst for a lifelong commitment to the power of language and emotion. Indeed, the writer has shared something personal, unique, and not previously revealed in her application. She has identified for the reader the moment of first inspiration—the exact source of her artistic expression.

The writer's internship provided the material for this prompt: "Tell us about your interest in your field of study."

Working with the small palate you are given, there's a certain balance between book knowledge and hand skills necessary to be a dentist." My mentor frequently repeated this piece of advice during my internship with him. Dr. Lizewski, our small town dentist, councilman, and former potato farmer, not only taught me about caps and crowns which he makes himself, but he also demonstrated how a vast amount of expertise is needed to work in the minuscule area of a tooth. It was no wonder that Dr. Lizewski, a man of many interests, strongly recommended that I enroll in his jewelry-making class to determine if I had the manual dexterity necessary for a career in dentistry. After attending numerous Monday night classes, I succeeded and have several beautiful bracelets to my credit, a bonus I never expected pursuing my interest in this profession!

Over the course of this internship, I realized how vital dentistry is in providing a service to enrich people's lives. Whether it be whitening teeth, filling cavities, or helping a senior with dentures, this dentist demonstrated his commitment to his profession. Being active in our town, Dr. Lizewski continually encourages and educates people about their health. Likewise, I aspire to this field not only for my own personal career development but also for a way to contribute to the community as a whole. Even though I have participated in many activities throughout the years, my internship with Dr. Lizewski has proven to be one of the most meaningful.

—Virginia Viviano

COMMENTS : Opening her response with a quotation from her mentor, this applicant immediately reveals the balance between her interest in dentistry and the human elements necessary to be successful. By placing him first in the essay, she honors her role model and recognizes the importance of his tutelage. She also indicates her preparation in the field prior to college, illustrating her commitment to her career choice. The strength of the response lies in the sensitivity of the student-teacher relationship. Here is a candidate who is cognizant of the technical training required, but one who has already decided that the personal touch is a far greater lesson to master. Her tribute to her inspirational mentor and her desire to follow in his mode speak to the reader of a mature and nurturing candidate.

In response to a question about "extracurricular activities and their influence," this student wrote:

There is no greater satisfaction than success in the face of hard work.
   I was a founding member of OBIES (Oyster Bay Internet Experience). OBIES developed after Charles Wang, CEO of Computer Associates, gave our school district a piece of property and a challenge to turn the space into a thriving business. We decided on an internet café. The amount of time we all dedicated to

OBIES was unheard of. I was also the project manager of OBIES and was responsible for contacting high power attorneys, communicating with politicians, designing business plans, balancing budgets, and many more tasks that the average high school student does not usually experience.

Furthermore, some of us even got to meet with Charles Wang and were asked to help the New York Islanders build part of their official website. It was exciting to work with a successful entrepreneur and with my favorite sports team. This was not an average high school experience.

It's good to know that after all my hard work OBIES is still standing and is now maintaining itself. It's even more elating to know that after I graduate, there will still be a piece of me in my community. I can't wait to go to college and expand my area of contributions to an even larger community.

—Ari Allen

COMMENTS : Even though a bit longer than the expected short response, this brief essay:
- ➤ Indicates a writer who is justifiably proud of his accomplishments
- ➤ Effectively describes the writer's role while acknowledging the participation of others in his achievement
- ➤ Makes a point of connecting the writer's high school experience to his potential in college

Last, but Certainly Not Least

Before moving on, we would like to give you some final pieces of advice. Here are four ideas to keep in mind as your essay evolves.

1. **Don't be afraid to begin *in medias res* (in the middle of things).** Plunge right into your situation if you feel comfortable doing so and IF it is appropriate to your purpose.

2. **Don't be afraid to pat yourself on the back.** Singing your own praises is perfectly acceptable. If you have been rewarded for an accomplishment, it is okay to tell your reader about it IF it is appropriate to the context of your essay. *But don't gloat, and avoid pomposity.*

3. **If you address a negative topic or issue, do your best to link it to a positive outcome or insight.**

4. **Choose one facet of an experience, and polish it for a single effect on the reader.** Let the reader feel inspired, amused, empathetic, appreciative, challenged, interested. Leave the reader wanting to know more about you.

THE EVOLVING ESSAY

Now that you've written the first draft of your application essay, we encourage you to take a break from it for a while. Put it aside for a day or two. You need to gain some objective distance.

When you're comfortable and decide it's time to take a closer look at your essay, we recommend that you follow the process we describe in this chapter.

Evaluating the First Draft
FOR A SENSE OF WHAT IT "SOUNDS" LIKE

Don't miss this step. Remember, the admissions reader wants to hear *your* voice. So in order to give yourself a sense of how others respond to your essay:

☑ Read your essay aloud to someone you trust, or if you feel daring, pick a person who doesn't know you too well.

☑ Observe the reactions of your listener:

- ➤ Smiles or frowns
- ➤ Nodding of head
- ➤ Furrowed brow
- ➤ Fidgeting
- ➤ Staring straight ahead
- ➤ Looking bored, picking lint off a sweater, etc.

Each of these reactions, and countless others, is an indication of the success or ineffectiveness of portions of your essay. **Do not skip this step.** Make adjustments accordingly.

FOR THE OVERALL PRESENTATION

This step in the editing and proofreading process is absolutely necessary. Either you or someone you trust needs to read the draft carefully to check for each of the following throughout the essay:

- ☑ Have you avoided the *laundry list presentation* (a chronology of events that reads like *first I did, then I did, next I saw,* etc.)?

- ☑ Have you avoided the *excuses syndrome* (*I would have been better, but...*)?

- ☑ Have you avoided *rambling* (going from one subject to another for no particular reason)?

- ☑ Does your entire essay *directly address the topic*?

- ☑ Have you chosen to use *language* (*diction*) *that is appropriate* for your purpose, topic, and audience?

- ☑ Have you avoided being or *becoming negative*? (*Don't do this. No way; not ever. Never!* We're referring to your tone, not your words.)

- ☑ Have you avoided *cutesiness*? Cutesiness can backfire on you. There's a fine line between cutesy and clever. If in doubt, leave it out. (For example, avoid using something like "a recipe for a successful college student: one cup of hard work, 2 tablespoons of extracurricular activities, a dash of spirit...") You get the idea. This may have been fresh once, but it is trite and ineffective now.)

- ☑ Have you avoided *sounding like a thesaurus*? (Use language you are familiar with and whose connotation and denotation you know. Nothing is more off-putting than reading a piece of writing that uses pompous and inappropriate words.)

- ☑ Have you checked the following:

- *Agreement of subject and verb*
- *Clarity of pronoun references* (*this, that, it, etc.*)
- *Punctuation*, including commas and apostrophes (*its* and *it's*—mistakes in this area signal a lackadaisical carelessness)
- *Tense consistency* (Once you choose a tense—present, past—stay with it. Switching tenses for no appropriate reason can be confusing to your reader.)
- *Transitions* [Is each of your paragraphs connected in some way to the preceding paragraph(s) and to the topic?]
- *Sentence variety* (Make certain to vary the way your sentences begin, the type of sentences, and the length of sentences. Sameness can quickly lead to boredom.)

☑ Have you established a *clear, consistent tone*?

- Formal or informal
- Serious or humorous
- Positive or negative
- Supportive or challenging

☑ Does your essay have a *clear voice*? (Your voice is your choice and involves your choice of topic, diction, organization, tone, details.)

FOR YOUR OPENING

The opening of your essay is the first "hello." The introduction has to make your intentions clear, grab your reader's interest, and imply both the organization and your relationship to your subject. With this in mind, check your opening for the following:

☑ Have you avoided beginning your essay with *simplistic and obvious sentences* like "I am going to talk about..." (this can be a sign of an immature writer) or "In my opinion..." (the reader knows you are giving your opinion)?

☑ Have you chosen to write an *explicit* or *implicit* opening? (See Chapter 4.)

☑ Do you *clearly indicate your topic* (without repeating the prompt)?

☑ Is the *technique* you use to introduce your essay specifically related to your purpose, subject, and audience?

- ➤ A quotation
- ➤ A piece of dialogue
- ➤ A rhetorical question
- ➤ A startling statement
- ➤ An engaging anecdote
- ➤ A challenge
- ➤ A revelation
- ➤ An interesting fact

FOR THE BODY OF YOUR ESSAY

The body of your essay develops the topic you've chosen to use in order to respond to a particular prompt or question. Each paragraph in the body of your essay has to move your reader closer to understanding the point you are making about your topic. You must be certain to show the interconnectedness among each of your major ideas and how they all relate to your main topic. To accomplish this, you need to check for the following:

☑ Does the body clearly follow an *organizational plan*?

☑ Narration (chronological? retrospective?)

☑ Description (spatial and/or sensory?)

☑ Contrast-comparison (subject by subject or point by point?)

☑ Explanation, analysis, cause and effect (least important to most important or vice versa?)

☑ For *each major point*, have you:

- ➤ Introduced it
- ➤ Described it
- ➤ Illustrated how it is related to your topic

☑ Are your *details accurate and appropriate* for your topic, purpose, and audience?

☑ Have you made certain that you have *transitions between paragraphs* to indicate the connection between the ideas?

☑ Do all your points specifically *relate to the prompt and the opening*?

☑ Is there *energy in your essay*, or is it flat?

FOR YOUR CONCLUSION

Once you've developed your subject in the body of your essay, you want the reader to leave your presentation understanding your subject and accepting your details in support of it. You also want the reader to sense a kind of closure and not feel as if he or she were left holding the bag. With that in mind, check following:

☑ Have you avoided the phrases *"In conclusion...,"* or *"Finally...,"* or *"In summary..."*?

☑ Have you chosen to write an *explicit* or *implicit* ending?

☑ Have you *linked the ending to something in the opening* of the essay?

☑ Have you *linked your essay (implicitly or explicitly) to the world of higher education*?

☑ Have you left the reader with a *sense of you as a person* who is interesting and thoughtful and who is a potentially positive contributor to campus life?

Once you or another person has checked your essay using the lists above, you are ready to do a very specifically directed reading that will examine the mechanics, form, style, and final impact of your personal essay.

 YOUR TURN

(Don't skip any of this.)

Mechanics

Have you checked:

_____ Spelling (Don't rely only on your computer's "spell check.")

_____ Punctuation

 _____ Apostrophes (It's difficult not to make a negative judgment when errors of this type appear. If in doubt, check your English handbook.)

 _____ Commas, periods, semicolons

 _____ Quotation marks (Use with direct quotations and short texts, poems—make certain to embed direct quotations and explain their connections to the main topic.)

 _____ Underlining or italicizing titles of books, movies, plays, magazines, etc.

_____ Sentence structure (Avoid fragments and run-ons.)

_____ Wording (Be careful not to leave words out or accidentally double up.)

_____ Tense (Use the same tense throughout unless there is a very good reason to change it.)

_____ Subject-verb agreement

_____ Paragraph indentation

_____ Number of words (Stay within a reasonable range of the requirement.)

Form

Have you:

_____ Engaged the reader with a strong opening

_____ Presented the reader with a clear thesis

_____ Chosen a tone that will convey your thoughts effectively

_____ Created a coherent structure for your essay

_____ Constructed a strong ending that leaves the reader wanting to meet you

_____ Proofread

Style

Have you checked to make certain that you have:

_____ Used vocabulary appropriate for your purpose

_____ Avoided sounding like a thesaurus

_____ Used diction (word choice) appropriate for the tone and subtext you wish to emphasize

_____ Included vivid and concrete images

_____ Used a variety of sentence structures

_____ Proofread

The Final Polish

Have you:

_____ Read your essay aloud to someone other than yourself

_____ "Read" between the lines for the subtext

_____ Put the essay away for a while and then taken a fresh look at it

_____ Connected your ideas to a universal application

_____ Proofread

NOTE: Be aware that many teachers will not be willing to either revise or change your essay. Just because someone reads your work does not mean he or she has proofread it and/or approved of it. *This is your responsibility.*

If you exceed the assigned word count, try to identify sections where you can economize your language further without damaging the overall effectiveness of the essay. If you're still over the word count, change the font size and fit the essay on one page.

FOR EXAMPLE

 Two million students writing over three million application essays. So many writers, so many goals and dreams. So many hopes, so much talent. So many questions.

We want you to have a realistic view of the competition out there. While perfect papers are thrilling to read and an admission officer's delight, let's be realistic. There are only so many valedictorians, English majors, and potential Pulitzer Prize winners among the millions. It's lonely at the top. And, yet, too often the perfect papers are the models students are expected to equal. How daunting and unrealistic this can be.

You must strive for your personal best, not someone else's, *yours*. But it's still valuable to get a picture of your competition. We've included a broad spectrum of genuine student essays that address a variety of prompts, illustrate wide-ranging experiences, and successfully introduce the writers to the college admissions readers.

You will meet students who present themselves as scholars, athletes, musicians, humanitarians, thinkers, risk takers, and just plain good kids. Their colleges run the gamut from the Ivy League to the local community college.

The essays and excerpts of essays that you will read in this chapter are REAL, warts and all. They are reprinted here as they were submitted.

Each of these student writers had different goals and different skills, but each faced a common challenge. Each of the student writers demonstrated his or her uniqueness through an essay that is personal and germane to that student. **ALL were successful.**

Following each essay is a brief commentary that highlights that essay's effectiveness.

When you read each essay, note how, as an objective reader, you "read" it:

➤ Become aware of what allowed this student to be successful.

➤ Which essays do you respond to?

➤ What is it that draws you to these essays?

➤ What qualities exhibited by these student writers can you incorporate into your own essay?

Remember, modeling does not mean copying. However, there are suggestions in the commentaries that can provide you with interesting approaches and guidelines, as well as patterns and styles you may decide you want to avoid.

Successful Essays

These essays in this section provide the reader with a genuine perspective on the uniqueness and individuality of the student writers. Although not perfect, the essays are effective. Keep in mind that perfection is not the goal here. The goal is communication, connection, and positive response.

The college admissions people are well versed in the lives of 17- and 18-year-olds. There's not much they haven't read about. They, too, are not expecting perfection, but they will not tolerate just a haphazard first draft. **Reading with the hope of getting a sense of who you are, the readers are on your side.**

We invite you to meet a group of student writers who successfully presented themselves to a wide variety of readers. See if you can envision the applicants as you listen to their voices. What can you infer about their strengths and weaknesses as candidates for admission?

Following each of the essays is a brief commentary with suggestions for you as a writer. Ask yourself if you concur with the commentator's remarks, and consider how the comments might apply to your own writing.

EXAMPLE ONE: PERSONAL INFLUENCE

The boys' bathroom filled with vaporized liquid nitrogen as Mr. Bennett kicked open the door and ran back to the classroom with our eighth period chemistry class sprinting behind him. After we safely found our way to our desks and the door sealed shut, we burst into laughter, relieved that the assistant principal had not sniffed us out. For most teachers, this experiment would be an unacceptable risk to their tenure, but for Mr. Bennett it was a learning experience for his students. The concept of separation of fun and learning did not apply to our honors chemistry class.

Honors Chemistry has long had an ominous reputation of being an *impossible* class along with being incredibly boring. Mr. Bennett allayed my fear of the class when I walked into Room 315 and saw him sitting back with his hands behind his head and his feet up on the desk, smiling and making jokes. I could tell that Mr. Bennett was not your average science teacher. And how right I was. The first few weeks of class consisted of the typical "Don't Burn Your Eyes Out" lectures and "How Well Can You Use a Graduated Cylinder" exercises. No, these were not thrilling, exhilarating lessons, but somehow Bennett, as we fondly called him, made them bearable. From joking around about how goofy everyone looked in the pink goggles to playing practical jokes on students, he taught us all we needed to know and made us laugh at the same time. To this day, I still remember to always measure to the bottom of the meniscus when using a graduated cylinder.

Bennett did not believe in textbooks. Although he went through the technical, required process of handing them out and writing down everyone's book number, that textbook remained in the bottom of my locker for the duration of the year where it suffered abuse and ripping from my other books. Bennett taught us the curriculum through entertaining, yet informative, lectures and practical labs. Previously, classes revolved around textbooks. However, Bennett's class taught me how to rely on my notes and what I had absorbed in class. Because he taught us so much using logic and observation, everything made sense.

One of the most important things that I have taken away from Bennett's class is the fact that learning can be greatly enhanced by humor and light-heartedness. Freezing oranges and saliva and tossing them out the window of our third floor classroom may seem like a waste of time to onlookers, but it was an effective way of making us remember the effects of liquid nitrogen. How else would I have remembered it two years later?

When Bennett told us to gather around the lab table and hold hands, we all thought we would be breaking into a version of Kumbaya. None of us knew what he was going to do, but knowing Mr. Bennett, it would be something that we were not expecting. Standing around the lab table, being played as fools by Bennett, we began to feel slight shocks, nothing harmful, running through our arms as the end student held the sink knob. We all jokingly shouted at Mr. Bennett who was teaching us that salt, added to water, was a conductor of electricity.

Bennett was a fan of food. Not only did he use food in an unconventional way during labs, he would also say, "I'll bet you an ice-cream," anytime we chose to argue with him about outcomes of demonstrations. Although we were victorious only once in a blue moon, needless to say, Bennett kept his promise. The day before winter break began, we all lethargically walked into the chemistry room with only sleep and 16 days of vacation on our minds. Mr. Bennett broke open the plastic wrapping of sugar cookies and twisted off the cap of a fruit punch container. He explained to us that we would be doing a lab on how many calories cookies and fruit punch contain. With that, he popped "Frosty the Snowman" in the VCR, and we broke into sighs of relief, followed by mad rushes to cookies.

I could always count on Bennett to make me laugh. As June approached and we began to feel the ominous presence of the REGENTS [exams] crawling toward us, Mr. Bennett decided to motivate our class by promising lunch for anyone who received a perfect score. Although it took twelve months to arrange our respective schedules, Bennett did not forget our deal. The following June, my friend Cheryl and I climbed into Bennett's pickup truck and made our way to the local pizzeria, the three of us reminiscing about the good ol' days of sneaking into the boys' bathroom and tossing frozen objects out the window.

—Erin Brown

COMMENTS: *The concept of separation of fun and learning did not apply to our honors chemistry class.* With this thematic statement the writer structures her tribute to her teacher. From its dramatic and amusing beginning, the rather long essay engages the reader and makes her wish she had had a teacher of this quality and spirit. But the essay is also successful because each detail that develops Bennett also unveils the spunk and astuteness of the writer.

While the text focuses on aspects of her teacher's influence, it also shows her values and attributes. Her sense of humor makes the essay soar. Specific details enliven the narrative: *How well can you use a graduated cylinder? Always measure to the bottom of the meniscus. Breaking into a version of Kumbaya.*

She connects her paragraphs with provocative statements that tempt the reader. *Bennett did not believe in textbooks. Bennett was a fan of food.* Who wouldn't want to read more? Her conclusion is especially effective because it manages to present one more Bennett treat, reveal that she had a perfect score on the Regents exam, connect the ending to the opening paragraph, and imbue the essay with the nostalgic and poignant sense that this was truly a unique individual in the writer's formative years. The reader can be fairly certain that the applicant will face life with humor and enthusiasm, scholarship and creativity, and appreciation for those who teach well.

EXAMPLE TWO: SELF-IDENTITY

The people speak my native tongue. The air is crisp and clean. Roads are infested with cows and wagons, and auto-rickshaws carry plump women. Cars whiz by as men race across the street. Children scream and yell as their mothers drag them from one shop to the next. Concession stands are on every corner selling somosas, gaolgopaes, and other common Indian cuisine.

My mother makes her way through the crowd of people into a clothing store. The men inside the store have refreshments ready and a spot saved just for her. I catch a glimpse of my father carrying ten bags of clothing. My brother and cousin take a couple of steps back out of the store before my mother can catch them.

I sit next to my mother; my father exhausted, grabs refreshment and sits to my right. Here I am in the middle of my parents, shopping! In America shopping with my parents I would be considered a "LOSER!" Yet here, shopping with parents is the norm and sometimes taken as an honor.

The man on the platform climbs up a series of shelves. He grabs a couple of traditional suits and jumps off the shelves onto the floor. I sit there in confusion; there is a ladder right behind the main door. I realize customs in India are different from those of America.

The man shows my parents stunning patterns of south Asia, from Punjabi suits to Hindu saris; every little design captures the beauty of India. A bright royal blue suit with gold trim catches my attention. I move towards the platform. I touch the suit, and it feels smooth against my skin.

The man wraps the suit in a plastic bag, while I attempt to find my brother. As I walk in the streets, I feel eyes on the back of my neck. I know they are looking at me because of my light skin color, rare in India. I keep walking, making sure not to turn and gather more attention.

This world is familiar but distant. My native country's customs are a different and complex adjustment. This moment in the clothing market gives me a perspective of my values. In India, our weddings are arranged and there is no room to fall in love before marriage, an ideal family vacation is to go to the clothing market, and a girl in her sophomore year of high school is usually expected to drop out and marry, and the same girl's future is nothing more than a housewife. Growing up in America has influenced my chances and values; they differ from those of my parents. I believe in love before marriage, and I don't enjoy going shopping with my mother let alone with my whole family. Yet the roots of my culture lie deep and I am incapable of totally disregarding my family's customs and tradition. The journey ahead will be more than interesting as I continue to define who I am.

—Tarnjit Devi

COMMENTS: A rush of vivid images greets the reader, creating an exotic setting for the essay. The opening is matter-of-fact in its declaration, *the people speak my native tongue.* Each detail illustrates precise diction and syntax. *Cars whiz, children scream, mothers drag* appear common enough, while *somosas* and *gaolgopaes* remind us we are not in familiar surroundings. The writer uses a simple and easy-to-identify-with event, shopping, to illustrate the contrast of two diverse ways of life. *The world is familiar but distant* provides insight into the speaker's complexity as she explores a balance in her personal quest for identity.

An interesting touch is how the writer mixes objective statements with personal activities, creating a sense of the speaker as both observer and participant and underscoring the motif of duality. *The man shows my parents stunning patterns of south Asia....*

I move towards the platform. I touch the suit, and it feels smooth against my skin.

The essay is successful because the reader is allowed to accompany the speaker on her journey to understanding and to another world, college.

☞ YOUR TURN ☜

Contrast two cultures and your role in each. Capture the flavor of the more exotic influence and take the reader with you as you interact in both worlds.

EXAMPLE THREE: SPORTS LESSON

I stepped up to the plate with one hand holding my helmet so it didn't fall off my head and the other holding up my pants while I tried to hold the heavy bat. My first few attempts at the plate as a little leaguer were unsuccessful, but I wouldn't give up. During my first six times up at bat I struck out, but the seventh time I hit a double. My perseverance paid off, and my eighth time up at bat I hit a home run. That would have been the ultimate if I had only known the correct order to *run the bases*.

This momentous event had a significant impact on my life. It taught me never to give up and to continue to push myself to reach my optimal potential. When I was in sixth grade, I took a placement test, and unfortunately, I was the only one of my friends who did not make it into the advanced classes. I was devastated, disappointed, and dismayed. During the next two weeks, I studied diligently for the class tests, proved to my teachers that I had the ability to move forward, and was placed into the advanced program that continued throughout my high school years.

I took this lesson and applied it not only to my scholastic life but also to my athletic pursuits. In July and August of 2001, I joined the city's Softball Summer Travel Team which was made up of the most valuable players in my town. To my disappointment, the coach didn't play me for the first three weeks because I was the youngest player on the team, and he doubted my ability. One day, the starter was injured, and I lucked out and was given a chance to play. The coach's jaw dropped when he saw me dive for the ball and tag out my opponent. From this moment on, he saw me through different eyes. I can distinctly remember the coach saying, "The cream rises to the top." This made me feel like I was someone special and that I had potential to fulfill any goal I set for myself. That summer the team demonstrated cooperative team efforts and ultimately placed second in the state.

As a student I have always had to balance my academic and sports lives and it was not always easy. My life followed the rituals of going to school, going to practice until the sun went down, and finally getting home to study and do homework feeling mentally and physically exhausted. Despite the rigorous schedule I have kept ever since seventh grade, I feel that balancing softball and academics has taught me what it takes to succeed and develop a strong work ethic.

Over the years, especially in high school, I have developed resiliency and the ability to bounce back after losing a game or not getting an <u>A</u>. In addition, I have learned the importance of balancing competition and fun so that my priorities are straight. I have also learned how to work well with others and to take constructive criticism.

I have been very fortunate to have coaches and teachers who have said to me that nothing is impossible, and these words continually reverberate in my ears. I welcome challenges, and whether I succeed is not as important as having tried and tested myself to achieve my own high standards. Derek Jeter, the New York Yankees' shortstop, may have copied the number two off my back, but I still strive to be number one!

—Jessica R. Frumer

COMMENTS: This essay, one that links sports and academics, is effective because it presents an authentic voice to the reader. It focuses on both the strengths and weaknesses of the applicant, tracing her growth as she diligently overcomes the challenges in her young life. Her honest portrayal indicates an applicant eager to learn and willing to take criticism. She modestly lets the reader know that which she is proudest of: her coach's assessment that *the cream rises to the top*. She is keenly aware of how important positive reinforcement is and how it motivates her to strive for excellence. The writer doesn't merely tell us her attributes; she illustrates them with details. Every point is on topic and linked with chronological connective tissue. Her perseverance and resiliency, aligned with her strong work ethic, make her a very desirable applicant. Her conclusion tempers the intensity of her situation with spirited humor. Move over Jeter—here she comes.

EXAMPLE FOUR: CONTRARY OPINION

In every high school across America, there is always the infamous group of star athletes. For whatever sport they play, they excel to a higher level of performance, many deemed the superstar. In and of itself, there is no detriment to such a viewpoint. But, is there a limit to the acknowledgement of these accomplishments? For every such star athlete who exists, there exist several students whose intelligence is just as impressive. However, there is no marching band that follows them, no cheering fans to celebrate their accomplishments, and no exorbitant monetary contract waiting for them.

As I prepare for college, I've witnessed many of these star athletes accept offers of admission from colleges which academically they have no justification for attending. Meanwhile, qualified, intelligent students are turned down at these same institutions. I do recognize the fiscal importance of athletics to colleges however. I'm well aware that one successful sports team could provide the budget for many of the college's activities. Promoting sports for fun and also for financial support is perfectly justified. The main problem is the lionizing of the athletes of these sports.

This problem only intensifies as I examine mainstream American life. Ask someone who the winning quarterback of a major football team is. Chances are they will know the answer. But, then ask them who is a leading doctor in cancer research. Ninety-nine times out of one hundred they won't have a clue. However, to their defense and my own, American society in general doesn't make it easy to know such information. On the cover of every newspaper there is always a sports figure. Nobel Prize winners are lucky if they make it on page twelve. In our land of freedom, people have a right to choose their own destiny. It's much more enjoyable to watch a basketball game than to watch a dissertation on a scientific discovery. Businessmen know this, and, as a result, athletics gain more attention than worthy alternatives. The impact of this trend is far-reaching, but is there any way to turn back the clock, or to at least mitigate the current problem?

I believe that there are many ways this situation can be curbed, but never eliminated. The sports philosophy is too far imbedded into our culture to simply wipe it out of existence. Certain measures, however, could turn the relationship of athletics and academics into a mutually beneficial one. With the tremendous amounts of revenue taken in from sporting events, colleges could support research more thoroughly. It would also be easier to encourage academic achievement if colleges more actively gave scholarships in this area. The key to correcting the current situation begins with the next generation of young people emerging as the leaders of our world. We have to be willing to initiate these changes and carry through with them. And, there's no better time to start affecting the future than the present.

—Brendan Kennedy

COMMENTS: This successful essay for Stanford University establishes the writer as an individual who is not afraid to express a contrary opinion or defend his thoughts against the mainstream. This individual is willing to risk presenting a critical analysis as his introduction to the reader because he obviously feels strongly about his subject and because he is confident he can craft a strong, meaningful argument to express his position.

The essay builds from the specific to the general and also from the immediate to the far-reaching. Each paragraph expands upon the original premise and develops the position with relevant details and conclusions.

The essay is developed in the following format:

Paragraph 1: Introduces the general problem: the high school athlete versus the scholar. The final sentence summarizes the situation: *However, there is no marching band that follows them, no cheering fans to celebrate their accomplishments, and no exorbitant monetary contract waiting for them.* The sentence itself is ordered from least to most important to emphasize the crux of the argument.

Paragraph 2: Personalizes the issue. The writer presents his specific observations, but now with regard to college admissions. This is the riskiest part of the essay, for it implies criticism of the very schools to which he is applying. Again, the concluding sentence carries the power: *The main problem is the lionizing of the athletes of these sports.*

Paragraph 3: Expands the topic to American values in general and provides challenging considerations for the reader. The final sentence moves the essay from the concrete to the hypothetical and philosophical conclusion. *The impact of this trend is far-reaching, but is there any way to turn back the clock, or to at least mitigate the current problem?*

Paragraph 4: Presents possibilities for a resolution of the problem. He links the two factions, athletics and academics, and urges his readers to address the issue now with action and change. *And, there's no better time to start affecting the future than the present.*

The tone of the essay—controlled, logical, concerned—goes a long way to making the words of the essay palatable for the reader. There is no assigned blame, whining, or ax grinding. Instead, there is the recognition of the circumstance and a resultant discussion. It is interesting to note that the writer is himself the recipient of several athletic scholarships to college for his swimming accomplishments; and perhaps, for this reason, he is able to offer a criticism of the very reward system he benefits from without sounding embittered.

EXAMPLE FIVE: VOLUNTEERISM

It was incredibly demanding physical labor, some days worse than others. The soreness of my body when waking up each morning was unbearable. The sun pounded on my face as I swung buckets of cement back and forth. This was all so foreign to me. Never having held a hammer in my life, I was now building a school with real cement and cinderblocks.

The excitement of the children's faces as the group of Americans walked by, the smell of poverty, the houses made of flattened tin cans; these are all images that struck me. Walking into a small village outside of La Vega, it is something one only sees on an infomercial for Save the Children. Getting a day off from work to interact with the children was a great opportunity. The delight, laughter, and huge smiles that lit up their faces when I handed them a picture I had drawn, one would think I had given them a $100 bill. They were the happiest children I had ever encountered. Even after attending their first medical clinic in years, the people, both children and adults, were happy. They were so appreciative of any help that was offered to them. For our group, it was a different story. We heard words like tuberculosis, AIDS, all sorts of viruses that many of us had never even heard of. Even the adults who were ill were still smiling. Never in my life did I imagine myself in this type of setting. For most of us it was something we had never seen. It was a hard hit of reality. Witnessing this gave me the drive to continue to work as hard as I could when I thought I could not go on any longer.

Working with 100 strangers from all over the country was spiritually uplifting. All were so different, cooperative, and energetic. Making up fun new songs while working became a daily ritual. Counting the cinderblocks while swinging them back and forth to one another was the encouragement we needed to reach our goal of 6000. When feeling tired and worn, I could always count on someone to tap me on the back and remind me why we were doing this. As an independent person, working cooperatively with a group was a huge step for me. In the beginning, it was hard to work as a group with everyone else, but day by day, it became more natural. It was an interesting revelation to me. Recognizing the needs of the people of La Vega and the needs of our group, it was all the same. People need each other, and it is inspirational knowing that I can make a difference in other people's lives.

—Joelle Soliman

COMMENTS: The writer's obvious sincerity and commitment are responsible for the impact of this essay. There is a wide-eyed naïveté that translates to the reader, and so we experience the metamorphosis of the writer as she shares her encounters with us. She reveals her personal changes as she learns firsthand about another way of life, one so foreign to her. Her introduction is effectively developed. She plunges right in, builds the images of the task, states her inexperience, and only then reveals her subject. By this point the reader is on the journey with her.

The most endearing aspect of this essay is its positive and uplifting tone. Instead of a litany of human suffering or a self-congratulatory valentine, the writer emphasizes the joy she experiences with the people she meets and through the work she contributes.

The candidate shows through myriad details her own evolution and indicates that she indeed learns by doing. She will undoubtedly be a receptive student, eager to participate, unafraid of hard work, and committed to making a difference.

☞ YOUR TURN ☜

Volunteer work is a strong subject for an essay because it allows you to write about what you do, where you do it, and how it affects others as well as you. Be careful—show the experience; don't just brag about your good deeds. Try to choose a small turning point in your efforts and polish it, rather than recounting the entire history of your experience.

EXAMPLE SIX: USING A METAPHOR, DESCRIBE LIFE

Conventionally, life is often compared to a footrace or a game of baseball. However, in a race, the same person can win repeatedly, and as the Yankees have shown, the same problem exists in baseball. I like to think of life in terms of chemistry, specifically, the Quantum Mechanical Model of the atom. With the goings-on of the world as the nucleus, we humans travel through life as electrons, each with varying degrees of certainty, excitement, and attachments.

As atoms strive to acquire stable configurations, they shed or gain electrons. Negativity is added when babies are born; electrons are released when children are relinquished to death, college, or become some combination of the two. Either sharing electrons or completely surrendering them to another, atoms join in union to form compounds that make life. Relationships are tantamount with the formation of bonds; similar interests lead to a date which leads to romance which leads to marriage—the ultimate covalent bond. If a divorce occurs, a bond is broken.

As either electrons or protons, people respectively repel and attract others. Angry, cynical, hermits repel the public—insisting to stay inside their minuscule cells, oriented as far from others as possible, thereby adhering to VSEPR Theory. In opposition, charismatic or altruistic individuals seek to better their environment through volunteer work, hospitable attitudes, and a general understanding of varied perspectives. Like most organizations, life contains its moderates and an atom contains its neutrons. As long as choices exist, indecisive or apathetic individuals will sit on the fence, not particularly agreeing with the indisputable hospitality of the protons or particularly disagreeing with the solitude cherished by electrons.

Life is uncertain. Not even the most accurate deck of Tarot cards can foretell the future in its entirety. In essence, just like atoms, life is subject to the terms of Heisenberg's Uncertainty Principle. Heisenberg stated that both the location and the momentum of an electron cannot be precisely known. Regardless of the events of the present, anything can happen. A driver might be instantaneously killed by a drunk driver, without having any intimation of what was to happen prior to or what happens afterwards. All present horrors and future glories are completely unforeseeable, as chance plays a hand in dictating the events of life. Like electrons, we can only give an approximation of what the future will hold and where we will be placed.

Separately, each classification and particle is insignificant. Only in the combination of all portions is the unit effective and productive. Without protons, no need for electrons would exist. In a sense, life is chemical equilibrium at its finest. There must be balance between the different aspects of life; some successes, some solitude, and some overabundance. Without each and every one of these items, a life wouldn't be complete. Similarly, the Massachusetts Institute of Technology will not be complete without the tiny little electron known as Elyse.

—Elyse Pieper

COMMENTS: This interesting response to a difficult prompt serves as a platform for the candidate to reveal many facets of her personality and academic strengths. She develops her extended metaphor in an ordered and rational manner. Each paragraph explores an aspect of her essential comparison: life as an electron, the world as atom.

Within the essay, she connects multiple chemistry terms with their specific counterparts in the world according to Elyse.

The essay is clever but not cutesy, and it continues to broaden in its scope. The structure moves from personal roles to relationships, choices, and uncertainties and then back to the opening, personal role—*the Massachusetts Institute of Technology will not be complete without the tiny little electron known as Elyse*.

This essay relies on the reader to extract what lies between the lines. The reader readily acknowledges the writer's scholarship and ability to develop an essay, but a more subtle picture also emerges. Here is an applicant who thinks outside the box and sees relationships between divergent properties. She considers social issues as well as scientific ones. She applies book learning to greater generalities about the human condition. She manages to inject a glimpse of her personality into an analytical exercise. Sounds like she's ready for the challenges of college.

☞ YOUR TURN ☜

Try your hand at an extended metaphor, or conceit. Read some first. Try the poem "The Author to Her Book" by Anne Bradstreet or "All the World's a Stage" (from *As You Like It*) by William Shakespeare. Make sure you have numerous points of comparison, and be sure to connect your essay to your value as a college applicant.

EXAMPLE SEVEN: ANALYZE AN APPEARANCE THAT DECEIVED YOU

As a generalization, the thought process of a rational person is: *think*, feel, act. An irrational person goes: *feel*, act, think. The main feeling that can cause a person to switch from rational to irrational is fear. With these two points of view, I tested my own character and learned how something that seemed to be so simple could be extremely difficult.

During the summer of 2003, I applied for and received a job at the Universal Studios Theme Park in Hollywood. When I took a job at Universal, I never imagined that I actually would have to think: just sweep and tear tickets. I started off as an Admissions Host (the official title for a ticket-taker) and quickly moved through two promotions to Assistant Lead of Tickets. With the advancement, came new responsibilities. I found myself placed in charge of counting large amounts of money; nearly 30,000 dollars went through my hands each day! Although I was handling huge amounts of money (and a hundred dollars could easily get lost), I had to remember not to let fear settle in because fear would make me do something irrational: a mistake. I had to remain calm and just let myself think, then I would act accordingly, and I did. My award was my own personal walkie-talkie, which happened to be the true sign of power. In addition, I was told to handle "guest situations." I was terrified; however, I was also astonished at how I handled these guest situations. From this grew a new and stronger Earle.

Handling the guest situations, forced me to step outside of my normal character. I do not have a very large stature. I am 5'5" (and hoping for more), slight of build, with the overall look of a thirteen year old. And at work I needed to learn how to tower over a 6'5" giant, how to out-muscle a huge 200-pound body builder, and out-wit a 23-year-old college graduate—all from behind a thin piece of glass. I had to go from an accommodating, nice, young man from Guest Relations to someone who was not going to give in no matter how much the guest yelled and screamed. Further, I had to remember to remain rational, not to let fear seep in because I could do it. I knew all of the answers; I had been there for two and half months. I had to remember that nervousness would be my demise and the only way to handle the situations was to be calm, cool, and confident. Of course the first situation was a challenge: a call over the radio informed me that Matthew had a problem. Matthew briefed me on why this woman was complaining. I took a deep breath and remembered to remain calm. Although I was terrified and shaking uncontrollably on the inside, the only thing that mattered was the confidence I showed to the guest. With that in mind, I walked up, argued with the woman and, astonishingly enough, resolved the situation.

The whole experience of working at Universal has better prepared me for my adventure in college. It has made me stronger and more able to hold myself up—despite looking young. I now know I can appear stronger, taller, and smarter than most people as along as I think I can, which is something that, until I worked at

Universal, I did not know I could do. For now as I travel off to college I know how to think, how to feel, how to act.

—Earle Le Masters IV

COMMENTS: This essay is successful because it:

> ➤ Answers the prompt in an implied and interesting manner
> ➤ Explores a candidate's growth from insecurity to confidence
> ➤ Provides insight into the specific experiences of an applicant
> ➤ Adheres to the prompt
> ➤ Is filled with concrete details and authentic references
> ➤ Has an "honest" and direct voice
> ➤ Presents an unassuming and self-aware portrait
> ➤ Takes the experience of the past, links it to the prompt, and expands the concept to the writer's future success

---

☞ YOUR TURN ☜

Write about a time when you were deceived by appearances or when you deceived others by your appearance.

EXAMPLE EIGHT: A RISK TAKER

At age three, I took my first steps across the balance beam. At age seven, I was entered into my first official gymnastics meet. At age fifteen, I earned the title of New York State vaulting champion in my age group. Yet, two months before turning the age of sixteen, I took one of the biggest risks of my life by leaving my lifelong gymnastics career behind.

Growing up, I was constantly identified as "the girl who did gymnastics." However, gymnastics means so much more to me than just something I "did." I devoted nearly all of my time, my energy, and my passion to the sport. Being a gymnast was a way of life for me and contributed significantly to the person I've grown to be. Practices were long and several times a week, leaving me little time for schoolwork. My gymnastics schedule kept me structured and taught me the fundamental importance of time management. Doing well in gymnastics and doing well in school went hand in hand; failure in either became unacceptable to me. Each new gymnastic skill I attempted to master required time and practice. When I did master a new skill, my senses of fulfillment, pride and accomplishment were my reward. From this, I learned values of hard work, patience, perseverance and dedication.

My life began changing around December of my sophomore year in high school. Although I was still continually improving as a gymnast and I could still feel my passion for the sport deep inside, the priorities in my life began to shift. Until that point in my life, I had always been content with my lack of involvement in school and community related activities, as well as my lack of a social life outside of the gym. However, it became increasingly hard to ignore the nagging feeling telling me I was no longer satisfied with being solely a gymnast. There were numerous activities and opportunities that were becoming progressively more appealing to me. During that month of December I came to the realization that I could not be both a competitive gymnast and the involved person I so desired to be. It was at this realization that I decided to take the risk of ending my thirteen year gymnastics career in search of the fulfillment I craved.

Adjusting to a new lifestyle excluding gymnastics was difficult at first, but with every new positive experience that came as a result of leaving gymnastics behind, the adjustment became easier. If I had been too afraid of taking a risk, I would never have known the enjoyment being a varsity athlete and representing my school could bring. Wearing my field hockey or lacrosse uniform and playing a team sport out on a field while working together with my teammates means something different to me because of what I gave up to be there. Being elected Vice President of the Leo Club, being an active participant in my student government, volunteering to help the causes of the American Cancer Society and the Long Island Chapter of the National Multiple Sclerosis Society, as well as most of the other activities I am involved with today, were all made possible by taking a risk.

There are days when a nostalgic feeling overwhelms me and I sit and reminisce about how my life has changed, though those days are far and few between. I made a difficult decision that December, took a risk, and altered the course of my life forever. I was given the best of two worlds. I was able to grow up doing something I loved and learning so much from it and then I was able to take what I learned and apply it to a different lifestyle. My success in school and in the various activities in which I am now involved is made possible by the foundation I was given through participating in gymnastics. I am who I am today largely because of the sport of gymnastics, even if gymnastics is no longer a part of my life today.

—Christine Poynter

COMMENTS: This is a very tightly written essay that exudes strength and confidence. The writer has taken a risk and literally changed the direction of her life, a major accomplishment. The readers receive thousands of essays about the impact of sports on young lives and the positive effects that athletics provide, but this is unique because the writer chooses to leave the world in which she has had much success and venture into previously unknown areas.

The essay begins as a list of impressive accomplishments, but they are only mentioned, not elaborated on. The emphasis is not on the gymnast, but on what she learned on her way to becoming *the girl who did gymnastics*. The writer makes it clear that her entire personality was governed by the restrictions and demands of excellence. *Doing well in gymnastics and doing well in school went hand in hand; failure in either became unacceptable to me.*

The focus of the essay now shifts to the essence of the risk— life after gymnastics. With honesty and maturity, the writer indicates her realization: she craved fulfillment of a deeper nature. She deftly incorporates the activities she has experienced as a result of her risk. The joy of a fuller life of learning, service, and sports has been made possible by her choice.

Her conclusion links her two worlds and acknowledges the relationship between them. *I am who I am today largely because of the sport of gymnastics, even if gymnastics is no longer a part of my life today*.

Here is a portrait of an applicant with a strong sense of self, one who is grounded in diligence, excellence, and self-determination. Any college would be proud to accept her.

EXAMPLE NINE: A SENSE OF PLACE

Out of the darkness of the night, the approaching headlights shine with a soft glare upon my face. The cars fly by distantly beneath me as I sit cross-legged on the porch overhang on the side of my house. From my bird's nest view of Sunrise Highway I can watch the nightly commuters driving East and West along Long Island as I pull my fleece blanket tightly around my shoulders, away from the frigid siding. The cold wind brushes across my cheeks as a shiver runs down my spine from the brisk autumn night weather. The pure night sky sprinkled with brilliant stars is a soothing portrait as I hang my head back against my layered sweatshirts and breathe the fresh air in deeply.

A stressful day always draws me to this ledge, an escape from my three brothers, the building pressure of college, and the constant ring of my cell phone. Concealed from the neighborhood road by the ancient oak tree, I am exposed only to the eyes of the natural wildlife of Swan Lake that leads into my backyard. In this miniature paradise, my own secret alcove, I do my best thinking. Simple contemplation, such as reevaluating my play in the previous night's lacrosse game, reassuring myself of my performance on the 6th period's AP Chemistry test, or even simply deciding what time I should wake up the next morning for the five mile Breast Cancer Walk at Jones Beach is easy as I relax to the soothing sounds of the lake nearby. Or, I can participate in deeper meditation as my mind tackles looming questions about life or drifts into meaningful thought about my dreams, hopes, and aspirations.

I jump as a loud horn blares from the nearby thoroughfare. Although rush hour is well over, a blur of automobiles continuously stream past. I wonder where the mass of people that pass by are headed or what they are thinking about at that moment. Contemplating their past, does this crowd appreciate their success in life, or would they change something if the chance were granted? Did they chase the dreams they had when they were younger? In such a fast paced world today, the dreams and faith we have within ourselves can sometimes be erased and obscured by the responsibilities and duties with which we are confronted. Too many times people caught up in the everyday rush miss out and allow their lives to overshadow their dreams. However, nothing is as real as a dream. They are legitimate and are capable of taking you in the air and above the storms, if only you'll let them. The world can change around you, but your dream does not have to. Let your dream consume your life, not your life devour your dream.

I am not sure what I want to do with my life, but I do know I want to be something great. In fifty years I want to be remembered—maybe for my beneficial work with third world countries, or as the doctor who found the cure for cancer, or even as the first woman President. Stretching out my legs, I look up at the picturesque sky as a shooting star races across the night sky. Anything is possible.

—Kari Andersen

COMMENTS: This essay, a lovely descriptive musing, is especially effective for the following reasons:

➤ Interesting sentence variety
➤ Vivid details and description
➤ Excellent use of phrases and clauses
➤ A precise, mature vocabulary
➤ Structure that moves from descriptive to informative to philosophical
➤ The subtext that reveals an applicant who is reflective, attuned to nature, capable of abstract thought, socially aware, and questioning
➤ The details that support her academic challenges, athletic strengths, charitable commitments, and relaxation techniques
➤ A smooth and tranquil tone that illustrates an applicant of composure and self-awareness
➤ A successful linking of a topic, a special place, with greater concerns
➤ A positive and optimistic final statement

Several of the sentences stand out as indicators of the writer's depth and skill:

> *In this miniature paradise, my own secret alcove, I do my best thinking.*

> *Nothing is as real as a dream. They are legitimate and capable of taking you in the air and above the storms, if only you'll let them.*

> *Let your dream consume your life, not your life devour your dream.*

EXAMPLE TEN: A CHALLENGE FACED

Sitting in the classroom, biting my nails, it happens. "Jeanne, you're up." Fear consumes me. As the only freshman in the room, it occurs to me—I am alone. These seniors are going to laugh. They are much better actors than I. After all, I am just 14 years old, a 9th grader. The teacher smiles; does she honestly expect me to get up in front of all of them? I am glued to my chair. I use my arms to try and lift my burdensome body. My legs fall heavy like two large chunks of heavy steel as I struggle to walk to the front of the room. The colossal weight of my first monologue rests on my shoulders. I feel the wall in the room getting closer and closer. My heart is pulsing at a rapid pace in my throat. I explore the room for some encouragement, anything—a smile, a warm effervescent face—anything. The faces are too blurry for me to make out their expressions. Then it hits me; I am holding the ace. I worked on this, rehearsed like a mad woman. I know that working hard always has positive results. My conscientious work ethic is going to pay off like it always does. Forget them. What is it my teacher said? Oh, yes, "Get into character; forget everything; they don't exist."

I am a woman; I have just lost my child. I miss her. (The people in the classroom blur. My fear disappears like the moon with the coming of the vibrant morning sun.) It should have been me; I should be dead, not my poor, beautiful baby. I start to battle to restrain the stream of tears. That frightened freshman disappears; the classroom is gone, and all I can think about is my innocent baby.

I do not know what happened during my monologue. I am not sure when I started speaking or what it was that I said. I am not even sure if I was there until

I snapped out of it. However, I do know that when I pulled myself out of that trance, those seniors had tears in their eyes, and I had tears in mine. I am not sure if there was applause. I don't remember what everyone said. All I could think about was that I did it. I got into character and I forgot myself. It was the most amazing feeling. I affected an audience, and there was something about this new found power that made me feel special.

—Jeanne Messerschmitt

COMMENTS: This essay is a delight for the reader for many reasons:

➤ The voice of the writer is loud and strong. It is so genuine, it is as if the writer were telling the story in the same room.

➤ The pacing and sentence structure capture the anxiety of the moment—short subject-verb sentences build the tension.

➤ The use of the first-person present tense pulls the reader into the immediacy of the experience. The writer contrasts this with the past tense in the conclusion.

➤ The essay has an established structure. The writer presents the challenge and reverses it—*Then it hits me; I am holding the ace*—and records the success that results.

➤ The writer includes metaphors and similes to make her point.

➤ Dialogue is incorporated to further the story line.

➤ The writer shows us her monologue by framing it between her anxiety and her triumph. We are her audience, and we, too, are affected by this special conclusion.

➤ Her essay is concise, focused, and appropriate for the prompt.

☞ YOUR TURN ☜

Choose an episode that you can show through detail, dialogue, and imagery. Do not tell us about it—take the reader there with you.

EXAMPLE ELEVEN: A CHARACTER SKETCH

My cousin Alyssa is one of the most accomplished and interesting people I know. When it comes to colorful characters, she is a screaming hot-pink, attention-grabbing bundle of energy. Yet she has the ability to appear as if she was not the one guilty of finishing off a full tray of chocolate-covered strawberries. Just because her face is covered in chocolate does not mean she is guilty of the crime. Remember, things are not always what they appear to be.

Each of Alyssa's endeavors are ideal examples of her everlasting vitality and of her simple aspiration to enjoy the present. Her passion for singing has earned her a solo in every school production she has performed in, and this love affair has extended to all areas of music—particularly to that little known band from Liverpool, the Beatles. According to her, "We All Live in a Yellow Submarine," have had a cup of tea with "Lucy in the Sky with Diamonds" and eventually have to just "Let It Be." Alyssa is also very cultural. Her determination to continuously speak with a British accent no matter where she is or what she's doing is extremely admirable. I have to admit that she is quite good at it, and words like "cheerio" instead of goodbye and "blimey" for whatever that is supposed to mean can be used at the drop of a hat. Not bad for a person who has never been across "the pond." She is also a skillful master of martial arts. She once battered a not-so-pleasant relative of mine using her weapon of choice—a black patent-leather shoe. Needless to say, that certain relative thought twice before she crossed pathways with this Jackie Chan again. This beating was, and still is, considered a victory for many of the other relatives in my family. So, I guess you could also call Alyssa a freedom fighter against horrid (her British is rubbing off on me) relatives.

Alyssa always has a spot on her town's softball and soccer teams. She has earned gold, silver, and bronze medals in an array of events, including the balance beam, freestyle interpretive dance, and various running events in the Olympics—the Special Olympics, that is. I should probably mention that Alyssa has Down Syndrome, but that does not really seem to matter. What she has accomplished is good enough for anybody, with or without a disability.

Alyssa's bubbly character may seem unique for someone with a disability, but that could not be farther from the truth. Inspired by Alyssa, I started volunteering at Camp Anchor, a camp for mentally and physically disabled children and adults that Alyssa also happens to attend. For the past three years I have spent six weeks every summer volunteering there, and I have yet to come across a camper who did not express the same enthusiasm and determination as Alyssa.

One person might look at a camp like Anchor and see a heartbreaking scene of people who are disabled, some so severely that they need help eating and going to the bathroom, and feel it is quite depressing. When I look at Anchor, I see people who are willing to work hard to overcome their challenges despite their disabilities, and I see people who will welcome any friend over to their lunch table. There is no need to feel sorry for them.

Their determination to never give up and their ability to love people unconditionally can hardly be considered grounds for sympathy. It is ironic that at times the "retarded" people are able to treat others with more respect and better manners than "normal" people.

I am sure you have realized that Alyssa is quite a remarkable person, with or without a disability. There are people I know who are middle-aged and have yet to do half the things Alyssa has done. I, for one, still cannot speak with a British accent and have yet to master Alyssa's skill in the "martial arts." I do not think I'll ever get a solo in any school production, and it is not likely I will make it to the Olympics. However, I do hope to emulate Alyssa's love of life and to always tackle any obstacle in my way just the way Alyssa would—with hard work and determination. But, "blimey," this essay must now end. I promised Alyssa I would be back in the "yellow submarine" before dinner-time. "Hey Jude" is coming to dinner. Cheerio!

—Jessica Restivo

COMMENTS: This essay, essentially a character sketch of the writer's cousin, is—in addition—a portrait of the writer, because each detail and episode reflects her values and goals, as well. The essay is endearing not only because of its subject but also because of the charming and light-hearted tone and style. The topic, which could easily become maudlin or patronizing, is lively instead, without a trace of pity. In fact, the writer does not even reveal her cousin's circumstance until well into the essay. The gentle humor that runs through the essay is so uniquely expressed that the reader often smiles and finds himself rooting for this lovable character. *Just because her face is covered in chocolate does not mean she is guilty of the crime. She once battered a not-so-pleasant relative of mine using her weapon of choice—a black patent-leather shoe.*

The essay uses the anecdotes about Alyssa to introduce the writer's feelings about disability and her own perceptions and problems. Her refusal to feel sorry for herself and her admiration for Alyssa have made her upbeat and determined to face life's challenges. Returning to the opening passages with the good humor that is at the heart of this applicant, the writer ends her essay whimsically.

EXAMPLE TWELVE: A PERSONAL CHARACTERISTIC

I think no virtue goes with size," wrote Ralph Waldo Emerson. Emerson is essentially saying that size does not matter and that is how I choose to live my life. Although I am short, I do not step down; I do not give in; and I am not pushed out of the way. I am a leader. I will not allow my height to stop me from doing anything, nor will I let my height suppress my leadership abilities.

I was at my doctor's office having my routine physical when the nurse came in to measure how much I had grown over the past year. Three rechecks of the scale confirmed that I had not grown since the last physical the year before. I remained at five feet, two inches for two years straight. As the nurse left the room, I didn't know what to think. Had I stopped growing? Could I continue to grow next year? As more and more questions raced through my head, I came to the realization that height is not an important part of me. Physical dimensions do not make me who I am; they do not show what my potential is.

As the physical quickly came to an end, my doctor looked at my chart, paused, looked at me, and said he believed that I was done growing. I was caught off guard, and my reaction was a simple, "Oh, okay." I knew that my height did not have a huge impact on the rest of my life. I was fortunate enough to have many wonderful things in life, and I hoped and continue to hope that being short will be the worst thing that ever happens to me. Following my comment, the doctor invited my mother in. He made the mistake of telling my mother in front of me that I would stand at a height of five feet, two inches probably for the rest of my life. My mother was in complete shock at the news and began to cry. I was upset for her, but it did not bother me as much as it did her. I was also shocked that such a minor physical detail hurt my mother that much. She immediately requested a bone-age analysis which later confirmed my doctor's thoughts.

When my father came home that night and learned of the news, he tried to comfort me by naming all of our short friends. I was already comfortable with the news. I knew I would be short, and I knew nothing could change that. But, more importantly, I knew that my height would not truly affect anything I wanted to do. My father also blocked a Saturday afternoon to watch the movie *Rudy* with me, the true story of a short man who achieved his goal of playing for the Notre Dame football team. His height and size did not matter; he was still able to play for the team because he had heart. He wanted something so badly that his physical dimensions could not stop him. I believe that I act in the same manner. I do not allow my physical size to stop me from learning and from participating. For example, in ninth grade I tried out for the high school swim team. After the first day I didn't want to go back; I was shocked at how big and strong the other swimmers were. My father and I joined a gym and worked out the rest of the year. When I was in tenth grade I went back for the swim team, and I have loved it ever since.

I choose to do whatever I want in life. I choose not to let my height hinder my progress. I am a leader for my peers not because I have a few titles in some clubs. My peers value me for who I am inside. They look to me for advice and for encouragement. However, I value myself not by the views of others but for the progression in my life into adulthood and my maturity. I know I can be whatever I want to be, that I can go wherever I want to go, and that I can live however I want to live without worrying about my height being a negative factor. Nobody measured me when I became treasurer of the Honor Society, and I didn't have to line up according to size to become president of the French Club or Future Business Leaders of America. I am proud of who I am and who I can become.

I believe Emerson to be correct in his thought that size has no virtues. My merits and courage stem from my mental and emotional strengths, not from my physical dimensions. No matter what obstacles I encounter in my life, I know that I will continue to stand tall and look up to new heights and higher levels of excellence.

—Josh Putterman

COMMENTS: Only a well-adjusted and mature applicant could write an essay about so personal an issue and treat it with insight and objectivity. This writer chooses to face the situation squarely in the introduction and to make it clear that he will keep it in perspective. His voice is clear, honest, and confident, and the result is an essay that indicates a strong candidate. The essay's strengths include:

➤ A wise choice of quotation and an effective incorporation of it into the meaning of the essay.

➤ The establishment of a personal credo: *I will not allow my height to stop me from doing anything, nor will I let my height suppress my leadership abilities.*

➤ A well-developed narrative, on topic, which reveals other aspects of the writer: *Physical dimensions do not make me who I am; they do not show what my potential is.*

➤ Details that allow the reader to infer more about the writer: a caring family, a sense of humor, an appreciative nature, a sense of priority.

➤ The use of a parallel situation to illustrate his circumstance. *My father also blocked a Saturday afternoon to watch the movie* Rudy *with me. …he was still able to play for the team because he had heart.*

➤ Examples to develop and prove his assertion.

➤ Focusing on the positive aspects of a perceived negative.

➤ Strong transitions.

➤ Clever insights: *Nobody measured me when I became treasurer of the Honor Society, and I didn't have to line up according to size to become president of the French Club or Future Business Leaders of America.*

➤ A reconnection to his introductory thesis. Both this essay and this candidate will be standing tall above the others.

☞ YOUR TURN ☜

Discuss a weakness, shortcoming, or negative aspect, and turn it into a positive insight, quality, or experience.

EXAMPLE THIRTEEN: DESCRIBE A PERSON WHO HAD A SIGNIFICANT INFLUENCE ON YOU

I only knew that his name was Fuzzy because it was printed in careful capital letters on the brim of his stained white hat. He always wore a bow tie and a plaid shirt that was too short at the arms and legs. He sold avocado-colored toasters out of a shopping cart from the steps of a bodega in town and spent afternoons sitting behind the dirty windows of the Laundromat. I noticed him because of the whites of his eyes, shiny and bright against his wrinkled, brown skin.

Fuzzy gave me the consistency I needed in my otherwise chaotic life. When I couldn't count on my family or friends, I could count on Fuzzy. He was always there for me, with a grin and a nod as I walked past his "home." Although our exchanges were limited, there was a mutual and unspoken friendship between us because we represented "the other side" of life to each other. His kindness was tangible, and his happy spirit unlimited. He bought me a hot chocolate with what little money he had when I was forced to walk home in the snow in only my basketball uniform. On Independence Day, I passed him lemonade and a sparkler, and he said, "Bless you, and keep lighting up Broadway with your smile."

He never tried to teach me anything, but somehow he taught me the most. Fuzzy represented all those people who didn't let their disadvantages get them down. Regardless of his situations, he remained content. Rather than blame his situation on his age or race, he simply did not place blame at all. He just lived, and he taught me to do the same.

Unfortunately, the day came when I walked past the Laundromat and stared blankly into spinning laundry. Rumors about his disappearance filled the girls' bathroom in between who kissed who and who threw the nicest party. Some said he had died; others swore he moved to California. Supposedly, he was a million-aire who gave all his money to his estranged daughter.

The mystery surrounding Fuzzy slowly died down as new and more exciting high school dramas occurred.

But, I remember him.

—Dana Van Pamelen

COMMENTS: This strong essay is extremely effective because of its sensitive and humanistic tone. The speaker is direct and to the point. Each paragraph begins clearly with the major point the writer wishes to communicate: *I only knew that his name was Fuzzy; Fuzzy gave me the consistency I needed; He never tried to teach me anything, but....* There is nothing extraneous to detract from her focus.

The vivid details of the character and the setting re-create the scene for the reader—*bow tie, avocado-colored toasters, bodega, lemonade, sparkler.*

The simple gesture of exchange in the second paragraph reveals the writer's understanding of the greater significance of the event. This insight is continued in the following paragraph where Fuzzy's implicit message is delineated.

The fourth paragraph raises Fuzzy to the status of urban myth, and the writer's poignant understanding of high school drama is beautifully expressed.

The conclusion, eloquent in its brevity, refers both to the prompt and to the insights of the contrasting ways of living she has witnessed. This wise and self-aware writer would be a welcome member of any college community.

Risk Takers

Some students have had experiences that affected them so greatly that they are compelled to incorporate them into their personal essays. Such essays include highly personal revelations, deeply held convictions, and contrary or unexpected subjects. These essays are not for everyone, so do not feel that your own essay must be of such high intensity.

The following writers took the risk of writing about a subject that could result in misinterpretation or rejection. Generally, however, the sincerity and passion of these writers lifts their essays from sensationalism to personal epiphanies. We trust, as they did, that the intelligent reader keeps an open mind and hears the authentic voices of the writers.

EXAMPLE ONE: I AM...

Most of my friends can tell me which of their parents gave them their height, eye color, or freckles (or lack thereof). I only have half of the puzzle. I was conceived by a surrogate mother, so half of my genes and ancestry are unknown to me. I only have knowledge of half of my ethnic background (Eastern European). For a long time, I had trouble identifying myself as Jewish, because although my parents are Jewish and I've been raised Jewish, my birth mother, Shari, is not.

When asked to define myself, I never felt that I could. I could tell people that I was a female, that I was funny, that I liked music. But I could never tell any interesting stories about my background, since I didn't know the full story. Half of my definition was lost inside a woman with whom I had no contact.

I used to wonder what I would have been like if I had grown up with Shari. I would have two older brothers. I would live in Spokane, Washington. I would probably go to a public school. Would I still be funny? Would I look or dress differently? Would I have similar friends? Would I like the same music? Would I still dance? These thoughts made me feel even more lost when it came to defining myself since Shari was not a part of my life.

The day that I was able to define myself finally came. It was September 13, 2002, when I received my first letter from Shari. I saw the envelope as the container of all the secrets that were Me. The letter turned out to be something even more valuable.

Her letter described a life completely different from my own. Her sons, ages 19 and 21, were still living at home. Neither of them had college educations. Being the daughter of two doctors and a girl who has been brought up to value education and independence as top priorities, this puzzled me. How could this woman, this Other Half of Me, be nothing like me?

It was that day that I realized that Shari and I led completely separate lives.

She did not hold me as a definition of who she was. She had moved on from the year that I was the most important part of her life.

Since then, I've realized that I am who I am because of the life I've lived, not because of genetics. I've lived a privileged life. I am creative. I enjoy goofy humor. I am a city girl. I am Jewish.

Yes, I still take note of the fact that my birth mother's extended family has no relation to me. Yes, I still wonder what my life would be like if I had grown up in Shari's household, as Shari's only daughter. But I have stopped wondering who I am. Because I already know.

—Rebecca Gitlin

COMMENTS: Some writers choose topics that are so personal that you might question why we have included them as models. The answer is simple—the essay is an exemplar not because of its content alone but because of its other more universal qualities. This essay immediately captures the reader's interest because of its sense of mystery. *I only have half of the puzzle.* The essay probes the effects of a provocative topic. *I was conceived by a surrogate mother.*

The writer constructs a dilemma that the reader can empathize with. *Half of my definition was lost inside a woman with whom I had no contact.* The writer then provides concrete and poignant evidence of her wonderings and questions about how her life could have been. *Would I still be funny? Would I still dance?*

At this point the essay shifts dramatically, and the reader is hooked deeper. *I saw the envelope as the container of all the secrets that were Me.*

Now our writer undergoes her epiphany. *How could this woman, this Other Half of Me, be nothing like me? She did not hold me as a definition of who she was. I've realized I am who I am because of the life I've lived, not because of genetics.* Her concluding statement is succinct and satisfying. *I have stopped wondering who I am. Because I already know.*

Direct, matter-of-fact in tone, honest, and insightful, this could easily be the outline for any search-for-identity work of literature. Didn't Oedipus, Hamlet, Huck, and Holden, all ponder similar questions? This universal experience is what makes this version a success.

```
┌─────────────────────────────────────────────────────────────────┐
│                                                                   │
│                    ☞ YOUR TURN ☜                                  │
│                                                                   │
│   Apply the structure of the model to an insight you have experienced. Let │
│   the reader in on the situation, your quest, your disappointment and sub-  │
│   sequent understanding. Mix objective and personal statements. Avoid sen-  │
│   timentality.                                                    │
│                                                                   │
└─────────────────────────────────────────────────────────────────┘
```

EXAMPLE TWO: CREATING AN EXTENDED METAPHOR

Abstract for "The SeanKmehra-Yale Experiment"

Yale University is a chemical that is always striving to select top students of the nation to maintain its reputation for excellence. However, every year it undergoes an "admissions process." *SeanKmehra* nanoparticles have been well characterized in literature. They possess favorable characteristics such as intelligence, motivation, and imagination. It is known from various studies that *SeanKmehra* nanoparticles successfully enhance the properties of various educational institutions. But little is known about the effect of these particles on *Yale University*.

I hypothesized that immersing *SeanKmehra* into an aqueous solution of *Yale University* would cause *Yale University* to experience an enhancement of its particles and facilitate its 2003 undergraduate admissions process.

I tested my hypothesis by first synthesizing *SeanKmehra* nanoparticles using a novel method developed by *Jericho High Industries*. In this process, particles were manufactured and refined over a period of four years. A core of *Seanium* atoms 3 nanometers wide was coated with leadership using the *Student Council method*. The particles were then exposed to a complex chemical system, consisting of various top-grade *extracurricular activities* and *achievements*, to provide improved structural integrity. The particles were also irradiated with intense beams of *writing skills* for optimal performance. Before experimentation, the particles underwent rigorous tests such as *AP*, *SAT*, and *ACT* to ensure the quality and purity of the substance.

After synthesis, solid *SeanKmehra* particles were dissolved in a liquid form of ambition, and 2mL of this solution were pipetted in 10mL of *Yale University*. The solution was vortexed for 30 seconds and shaken vigorously until the bonding of *SeanKmehra* and *Yale University* particles was obvious, causing an increase in viscosity and change in color of the solution. This *SeanKmehra-Yale* composite was then allowed to settle and annealed for 4 years in a New Haven, Inc. oven at 23 degrees C. The sample was subsequently analyzed using optimal microscopy.

Under 100x magnification, *SeanKmehra* particles appeared to have escaped bondage with *Yale University* particles, but not before leaving a lasting impact on the *Yale* particles. Closer investigation at 500x magnification showed that, after 4 years, *SeanKmehra* nanoparticles caused a permanent conformational change in the *Yale University* particles. *Yale University* had now transformed into a superior form of itself, possessing enhanced characteristics, including better undergraduate science research, writing, and cultural diversity programs. Similarly, a complementary effect was observed on *SeanKmehra*; *Yale University* left its own mark on these nanoparticles. Not only were the aforementioned properties such as intelligence, motivation, and imagination enhanced, but so were a variety of properties, such as leadership, communication skills, knowledge, and charisma. This makes *SeanKmehra* an ideal nanoparticle for real-world commercial applications in industrial, medical, and scientific fields. I propose that the cause of this positive change might be *SeanKmehra*'s large affinity for success, a crucial part of the *Yale* molecule. Together, the compound creates a synergistic effect that improves both substances physically and chemically.

Future studies may involve immersing *SeanKmehra* particles into different forms of *Yale* molecules modified with varying functional groups or "schools," such as *graduate* or *medical*.

—Sean K. Mehra

COMMENTS: From its clever title to its clever conclusion, this essay remains in character. Here is an extended metaphor of the highest order. Although its readability is at times strained, it is because of the strict adherence to a scientific and objective tone and diction. It is this tone that unifies the essay and furthers its analogy. The language is elevated and formal, mimicking a genuine experiment. Indeed, choosing a college is an experiment, and using the scientific method to explore that choice is a unique approach.

This writer is obviously well versed in advanced science, but he is also well skilled in English. The vocabulary is precise and academic.

He speaks to his audience as those who will understand the nuances of his comparison. The essay is clearly structured and smoothly transitioned. His syntax is complex and varied. The examples and details are real and logically developed. The concept works.

The writer is clearly one who is willing to take a risk because the reader has to work a little harder to get to know the applicant than in most essays. But that strong voice comes through loud and clear. The essay is liberally sprinkled with humor and satire, both obvious and subtle. Nothing escapes observation, from SAT scores to the attributes and needs of Yale University.

The conclusion extends the metaphor outward: our candidate is applying for undergrad status, but he is already hypothesizing about medical school. Truly a forward thinker.

EXAMPLE THREE: AN INSIGHT

I approached the house with trepidation. I unlatched the lock on the cold steel fence and walked up the steps to the front door. Once inside the house, I smelled the familiar stench of liquor in the air. As I walked down the steps to my father's basement apartment, the odor grew stronger. There was my father asleep clutching the bottle in his arms as if it were his child.

My father is the motivation and inspiration in my life. Even while my mother was living, I was always daddy's little girl. Ever since sickle cell anemia claimed my mother's life when I was seven years old, my father has fallen victim to alcoholism. Unable to cope with his loss, he turned to alcohol as a problem-solver. When he lost his job, he entered the hospital only to return home and resume the same old debilitating habits. Without an occupation, my father was not able to continue payments to my private school. So, when I reached my sophomore year, I enrolled in our local high school. It was difficult to adapt to a new environment. My father felt terribly guilty for putting me through this and assured me that one day he would overcome this disease and everything would be better.

With my father not being able to take care of himself and definitely not able to perform his parental duties, I assumed the roles of both parent and child. I had to be responsible for budgeting our money (living off my mother's social security checks was tough). I also had to set my own restrictions and rules to live by. I cooked, cleaned, and managed other household tasks. Stress at home drove me to work harder in school. I doubled the workload by taking classes in both day and night school, and I completed both my junior and senior years simultaneously. In between day and night school I continued working with my father. I read literature to him, placed reminders around the house, and communicated with him daily to keep him focused on sobriety, all the while keeping up my school work and maintaining honors status. My father was the one who instilled in me the belief that no matter how hard life becomes, failure should never be an option.

My father is a blessing in my life. I know now that going through life with my father has made me the ambitious person I am today. Although he has caused me pain, it's his unconditional love and inspiration that drives me every day. If it weren't for my father, I would never have known the measure of my strength.

—Nicole Duke

COMMENTS: Honest but not sentimental. Brutally frank but fiercely loving. This essay's strength comes from the writer's ability to present her *unconditional love* for her father despite the manifestations of his illness.

The opening paragraph immediately engages the reader and indicates a young writer with a literary sensibility. The diction clearly establishes a conflict with the parent-child relationship: *trepidation, lock, cold steel, familiar stench, basement, odor, clutching*. In contrast, the opening of the second paragraph reveals the writer's heart. *My father is the motivation and inspiration in my life.* Here is an applicant who is a survivor with a mature take on life. And yet, she is not a complainer. She finds instead *the measure of her strength* in the struggles and assurances of her father.

The writer pares down to the bone the essence of her message to the reader: *My father was the one who instilled in me the belief that no matter how hard life becomes, failure should never be an option.*

This is a candidate who has met challenges and has endured and prevailed.

EXAMPLE FOUR: A LIFE-CHANGING EXPERIENCE

Throughout life people wonder why they are here, what their purpose is. Luckily, I have discovered my own answers to these questions at a very young age. Ralph Waldo Emerson once wrote "success [is]... to leave the world a bit better, whether by a healthy child, a garden patch or a redeemed social condition." I have been given the opportunity to know that I was placed here on Earth to be "successful," to give two wonderful people the greatest gift of all: a child.

Just months before my sixteenth birthday I had to face what I thought would be the worst thing to ever happen to me. I WAS PREGNANT. I vividly remember how afraid I was; thoughts ran through my head, "I can't have a kid, I'm only a kid myself! How can I be so stupid?! How could I make such a huge mistake?" All my boyfriend could do was to try to comfort me, as I obsessed over how my life and dreams were about to crumble into pieces.

Coming back to reality, I became preoccupied with the daunting question, "What will I do with this child—*my* child? I wanted my baby to have the best life possible, the life I could not give her. She needed parents who could take care of her and keep a roof over her head, who could feed her and keep clothes on her back, but most of all, a mother and father who could love her with an undying devotion. After much of my own consideration, and out of complete love for my baby, I searched for a Lutheran couple that wanted to adopt. Having made this decision, there was no turning back; I believe it would be the cruelest thing to get a couple's hopes up and then deny them their child—their own dream—in the very end. It would be like killing them.

It was by God's grace that I found the "perfect" Lutheran couple, despite the brevity of my search.

Throughout the pregnancy I came to know the adoptive parents, Karen and Bill, not just as friends, but as family. To both my boyfriend and me, Karen and Bill seemed too good to be true; the only thing missing in their life was a child. There would no longer be emptiness in their life; it was my duty to fill that hole of darkness with the light of a new-born baby. As the due date came closer, together we decided a name for our baby girl: Katherine Grace. However at the same time I became frightened.

How could I give away my first child?

How could I just let her go?

On the day of Katherine Grace's birth (February 22, 2003), I knew how I could give her away; I knew that I wasn't letting her go. I have never seen anyone happier than when I saw Karen and Bill looking at what God blessed them with, what God blesses each and every one of us with every day—LIFE. Seeing their faces assured me that I wasn't just giving baby Katherine away; I knew I was giving her everything I could possibly have hoped for her to have. That was enough for me.

As it turns out, this wasn't the worst thing that could ever happen; it was the best. Ever since my daughter's birth, I have thanked God for the miraculous things He does, and I will continue to thank Him for the rest of my life. I have been blessed with being able to get out of bed every morning knowing that three people's lives are better because of me. That is the best feeling in the world— *to know even one life has breathed easier because you have lived; [and] this is to have succeeded.*

—Heather Nathan

COMMENTS: This is an example of an essay that takes a risk. The topic is extremely personal and of a sensitive nature, and yet it is these qualities that also give the essay its strength. While we would not generally recommend such a confessional topic, it is the passionate faith and unwavering honesty of the writing that transcend the difficulty of the subject. The reader will be able to see beyond the specific circumstances and meet the mature young woman who overcame a challenge with grace, dignity, and courage.

In addition, the essay works because the author has chosen a narrative structure and earnest tone to communicate her ideas. She:

➤ Opens with a general statement about people and purpose and then moves to her specific purpose

➤ Uses an appropriate quotation to illustrate her thoughts and situation

➤ Moves from positive to negative to positive

➤ Avoids seeking sympathy or approval

➤ Allows the reader to follow her thought processes and conclusions

➤ Reveals her spiritual commitment and strength

➤ Shows her selflessness and connects it to a desire to do the right thing under pressure

EXAMPLE FIVE: CONTROVERSIAL ISSUE

I accept all people and advocate against intolerance, but I have not always felt this way. Several experiences and encounters have changed me.

Race has played a role in my own struggle for self-acceptance and tolerance. While my mother's background is European Jewish, my father was born and raised in Swaziland, Africa. After receiving his doctorate in Comparative Education, Baba was summoned by King Mswati III to be a cabinet minister. When I visited Swaziland with him at age 12, it was the first time I lived and went to school in a mainly black environment. Because I am black, I did not stand out except for my accent and unfamiliarity with Swazi culture. But, in the United States, through second grade, I attended an almost entirely white school where I encountered racism. When playing, some classmates told me I could not "be" our music teacher who was white or play sister with my white friends. Though I did not know why they said what they did, I knew it was wrong and told my Mom. My Mom and I donated a book to the class library called *Amazing Grace,* about a girl who overcomes racism and sexism at school to play the role of Peter Pan. We read it aloud at circle time to educate the other students about how everyone deserves equal treatment.

My parents made it clear that I could be anything I wanted to be, igniting my identification as a beautiful blend of black, white, Jewish, and African. But, like the narrator in Ralph Ellison's novel, *Invisible Man*, I find that both black and white people sometimes have trouble seeing all of me. For example, during my freshman year in high school, a black girl told me that I was "disadvantaged and confused" about my race and that interracial couples should spare their children by not having any. She called me an "Oreo." Sure, it made me angry, but I try to be a bridge between races, connecting different people, educating people from one race about the other and disproving stereotypes.

—Rebecca Frank

COMMENTS: This writer's forthright discussion is told with a maturity that belies the pain that frames the experiences in her background. The anecdote about her mother and the book indicates a level of trust and openness between mother and daughter. Rather than turn a mitigating event into a negative diatribe about racism, the writer and her mother choose to turn it into a learning experience for her community.

With this level of insight, this writer can truly be anything she wants to be.

Sparklers

We come now to the essays we all wish we could have written. Keep in mind Robert Browning's adage, "A man's reach should exceed his grasp." Let's face it; there are writers, and there are **writers!**

Spend some time with these student wordsmiths. Be impressed. Be awed. But *don't* be daunted. The admissions staff know that these essays are the exception, not the rule. Still, you can pick up some tips from these sparklers that may be able to light up your own essays.

EXAMPLE ONE: A PERSONAL INSIGHT—WHY I WRITE

It doesn't help to say I write because I feel I couldn't live without it. But I do. Yet in the same way that people question the meaning of life, I question not the meaning of my writing, but I question the cause. Why are my invariably purple pens drawn to the paper, or more aptly, why are my vulnerable fingers lured toward the keyboard? How is it that such a seemingly impersonal byproduct of the information age has such power to create? So writing does have the power to transcend the everyday.

So let's start in the negative. When I don't write, I'm miserable. Not outwardly, more of that grey-cloud, melancholy sort of thing.

Maybe I can't answer this question yet.

I write because I have something to *say*. I have something to say and I want to be heard. Maybe those who know me would say that it's not in my nature to be so direct, forthcoming, with my words, my attitude. Why what I have to say is more important than what someone else wants to say, I don't know. But I'm saying it. I'm a thinker; I'm an observer. I'm happy sitting on the sidewalk for an afternoon and just watching the people go by. Maybe that's the passivity. But the action comes through the words. This sort of underworld of personality. Drama lovers act, so they say, because it gives them the freedom to be whoever they want to be; it's an excuse to step out of their personality and temporarily escape the life that they lead. They have the luxury of hiding behind their characters. Part of me wishes that I could hide behind my words; the other part wishes that I had the courage to stand beside them.

All the same, we get to invent. You see these black squiggles on the page? They mean something to someone. They hold so much more than the barely three-dimensional piece of paper you are holding. I made these squiggles. This is part of my masterpiece, my growing body of work. The shape of the black ink is my sculpture.

Let's make writing and breathing interchangeable, just for a minute, operating under the hyperbolic assumption that this writer must write to live in the same way that she must breathe to live. *Meditation: focused breathing* becomes *Meditation: focused writing*. Find your center, face the day. To write is to discover parts we don't even know we have.

Sometimes I just sit down and my fingers start to move, and before I know it I read what I've written and I begin to cry. I haven't written the words. The words, as some would say, have written me.

If I can control these black squiggles of ink then maybe I can control something in my life. We writers play God—and I knew that before I ever knew who Faulkner was. We can mix, match, invent, delete. Babies are made of forty-six chromosomes, but literary masterpieces are allotted only 26 letters. That's it. That's all we get. But I'd say we do a pretty good job.

—Lara Friedrich

COMMENTS: *Why I write.* Instantly we are drawn into the essay, curious to hear the answer to the implied question, and answer it the writer does—with style and flair and a conversational voice that makes readers feel they are in the same room with her. Every statement enforces the power of the process on the writer. She evolves with the essay, telling the reader that *maybe I can't answer this question yet.* But on she goes, with deep, flowing sentences and thoughts until her great line: *Part of me wishes that I could hide behind my words; the other part wishes that I had the courage to stand beside them.*

She does become courageous in the next paragraph, claiming ownership for the squiggles, her masterpiece, her sculpture. This synthesis continues as she literally interchanges breathing and writing—stressing the essence of her personality. Another balanced sentence follows: *I haven't written the words...the words have written me.*

The creativity and exuberance of the writer overflows in the final statement. She is creator, artist, mystic, proud parent, and humble student. *Only 26 letters?* More than enough for her to win a spot at the college of her choice.

EXAMPLE TWO: PERSONAL INFLUENCE

That's the way it was with Churchill and Roosevelt. The same for Pierre and Madame Curie, or Watson and Crick. Ideological partners and collaborators, a relationship of mutual respect." When my Zaide spoke, I listened. When Bubbe spoke, well, that's a whole different story, but usually one told with a smile on my face and a chuckle in my voice.

It was my favorite time of the summer, that last week in August when I traveled upstate to Lake Louise Marie to spend quality time with my grandparents. Their country home was idyllic, rustic yet refined. My Zaide (grandfather) took great pride in his country home with its award-winning, manicured lawn and sturdy, boulder-reinforced bulkhead. The family legend has it he carried each and every one of these great rocks to their final resting place in his dilapidated wheelbarrow. No one else could do it "just right."

The serene lake shone like a polished mirror on those quiet sunsets, so quiet, in fact, that I could hear the fish jumping from the waters to catch their insect dinners. The surrounding woods were an adventure in symbiotic ecology. We spent many a day hiking around looking for "free" shrubbery that could be transplanted onto his property. For nourishment we would feast on wild berries; for a treat we would chew on wild sassafras root.

My Zaide is such a special man, although few people recognize that fact. Short and stocky with a barrel chest full of curling hair, his strength of body never goes unnoticed, but his strength of mind and character is what attracts me most to him. In his early years, he lived a difficult life, surviving the Great Depression in a broken home, thrust into the role of patriarch at the age of twelve, living a life of near poverty yet one rich in texture. He made his own way through college, the armed forces, and professional school, while still caring for the rest of the family. Zaide never had time for himself, except to read. That was his great passion...learning...everything! The man seems to have knowledge and insights into everything, and that is the basis for our most wonderful affinity. In the poorly lit den of his country retreat, away from the encumbrances that complicate the parent/child relationship, I am free to explore intellectual topics with a man of personal history, a survivor, a scientist, a student of philosophy.

With its dark hardwood floors warmed by the crackling fireplace and scattered Oriental rugs, and walls covered with photographs of places and people past, the den is where we collaborate. Delicate antique porcelains with fine latticework and muted colors; the sparkling samovar with its service for eight; florentined statuettes and figurines from far-off places; shimmering crystals which in the daylight cast rainbows upon the buttressed ceiling...these are his trophies, each of which evokes a tale steeped in history. I think to myself, those eyes have seen it all.

Those shimmering hazel eyes are my portals. As I gaze into them, I see so many things, not the least of which is his genuine love for me. However, his love is not the requisite love, not the love one routinely expects from kin, but rather the love one shares with a comrade-in-arms. When we confer in the den of reason, I am, in his eyes, an equal for whom he has the utmost respect. Though my years limit my exposure, he nonetheless cherishes my opinion on matters current or past. He wants to know what's on my mind and how I come to my conclusions. Did I use the scientific method in reaching my decision, or am I basing it on historical precedent? He values my perspective. I can relate to him in a manner in which I could never achieve with my too-close parents. Our discourses are ones of rationalism, not the harried affairs of home.

With its dusty, leather-bound books, roll-top desk, and antique analog radio, the den could just as well have been the perfect setting for Roosevelt and Churchill to debate the fate of the modern world. Perhaps, here, Watson and Crick could have finally put together the last pieces of that puzzling double helix they called DNA. Here, the Curies could have exclaimed *voila!* But, they all missed the chance by living in their own times. This special arena is ours, belonging to my Zaide and me. It is our fortress of solitude and resolve, where men of mutual respect and admiration can think and speak freely to explore the world and its marveled past and its infinite future.

—Jeremy Price

COMMENTS: This essay, which begins *in medias res*, immediately establishes its tone and subject. *When Zaide spoke, I listened.* The writer fills his gentle and nostalgic portrait with concrete details that provide a visual feast for the reader. The description of the scene is like the grandfather—rustic, yet refined. The image of him carrying the boulders imbues him with the power the writer wishes to convey. This power is far more lasting than his physical presence. The essay links the retreat with the freedom necessary to explore great ideas as equals, away from the interference of traditional roles and expectations.

Once again the diction sets the mood of the piece. *The scattered Oriental rugs, delicate antique porcelains with fine latticework, the sparkling samovar, florentined statuettes and figurines, the buttressed ceiling,* etc., evoke the magical past and rich memories the writer shares with his subject.

Wisely, the writer moves from the descriptive to the analytical section of the essay as he probes the questions of love and life and opens the essay to a more universal applicability. The insight *he values my perspective* makes us wish to know more about the writer and his views.

The essay concludes with wonderful details and returns to the opening parallels—Roosevelt, Churchill, et al., and the reader feels privileged to have shared that *special arena* with the writer and his grandfather.

Try to link a special locale with a particular subject. Intertwine the images of place, person, and purpose. The essay will ring true if you base it on a real person in a genuine setting. Once you establish the details, you can impose your ideas on the structure. Remember *The Old Man and the Sea*? Or think of a small setting and make it crystal clear to the reader—a setting like your school locker and what it reveals about you. Then expand the concept to a broader context, e.g., organized, eclectic, a repository of self or curiously empty, waiting to be filled.

EXAMPLE THREE: FAMILY

Katrina's—stick straight golden; Genevieve's—wavy black; mine—curly chestnut. Our contrasting hair colors are only the beginning of the differences that scream: "Are you really sisters?!" My two adopted sisters and a dozen adopted cousins hail from different continents and share few roots and physical features. Yet, the ties of faith and loyalty that bind us would defy the best of the Kennedys and Osmonds.

Growing up with two older siblings with whom I share no common DNA has given me a wonderful avenue of opportunity. The first-born, Genevieve is our resident massage therapist, retro hippie and vegetarian. Her gentle presence always soothes my soul and our discussions exercise my mind. Although we have completely different views on everything from Prada to Putin, she is one of my best friends. Katrina is the size zero hyperactive child. She and I are still trying to find that tiny thread of mutual interest to re-ignite our childhood bond. We've shared cribs, strollers, Happy Meals and my mom's attention for much of our youth, but for now seem to be traveling diverse paths. Only 18 months apart, we have always preferred to emphasize our opposing opinions and participate in regular verbal sparring matches. Yet, when she fell and broke her arm a couple of years ago, I had no trouble tying her shoes for six weeks.

My bio would involve taking descriptions of my sisters and turning them inside out. As their only biological child, I am a picture of my parents. I confess to being a sort of nerd, a pretty good athlete, a chatter-box, poet, comedian and perfectionist. As a GAP poster child, family-reunion coordinator, and by far the most stubborn member of my family, I add the finishing touches to our trio of dissimilarities. Fate made me the surprise third child, who sitting down to write her college essay realizes how her family has defined her.

Understanding and accepting members of our diverse clan, with their occasional frailties, language barriers and vague ancestries, could prove challenging at times, but it has made difference a thing of beauty and an education in itself. It has encouraged cooperation, charity and curiosity. Ironically, this people-web of ours has rendered me a sort of minority. No one can claim superiority here. We are just a great bunch of individuals who care about one another. So, when our family decided to host Kira, a 10-year-old Russian orphan this past summer, it was as if she had been here all along. I guess it was because there are just no strict qualifications for being a Wissemann. If you can spell it, you're in.

I take my unique family very seriously and boast of it proudly. Being a member has continuously taught me that everyone has something to offer and that the single, basic, universal truth involves simply doing the right thing. Some of this is fun, and some is obligation. Most of it is love.

—Hilary Wissemann

COMMENTS: The author of this essay chooses to present herself in the context of her unique siblings. By highlighting the physical disparities that exist in her family, she emphasizes instead the ethical and emotional commonalities that bind them together. She structures her essay from a general statement: *Yet, the ties of faith and loyalty that bind us would defy the best of the Kennedys and Osmonds*, and continues with specifics that illustrate the individuality of her clan. She lifts the essay in the final paragraph when she explains how the diversity of her surroundings has equipped her to meet challenges, to cooperate, and to be charitable.

Her warm and welcoming invitation to join her loving family reveals her heartfelt appreciation for the fortunate circumstances of her upbringing. Here is a portrait of a young woman who is introspective, comfortable with herself, open to others, secure in her place, and willing to be even more expansive in her future. This is not a romanticized and sugary portrait of an idealized family, but rather a genuine glimpse into an interesting candidate's biography.

This essay so impressed the admissions officers at Lafayette College that they sent the writer a letter praising her essay.

☞ **YOUR TURN** ☜

Try describing yourself in terms of your family or group of friends. Do a thorough analysis—include common threads and differences. Use contrast as a tool rather than relying heavily on comparison.

EXAMPLE FOUR: CREATIVE THINKING

Simplify, Simplify, Simplify

It is all very well for Henry David Thoreau, on the clear banks of Walden Pond to proclaim the evils of materialism, but to do so without examining the full subtleties of his environment would be folly. In truth, the man lived with untold riches, reaping their benefit at every moment. No, he did not boast a secret stash of Prada shoes or French champagne—his possessions were not physical objects he shared a transient relationship with, but things he owned wholly, only lost upon death. A man's true possessions are his words and the ideals they embody. And so here I take Thoreau's advice a step further and pare down not VCR's and writing desks, but those belongings I treasure most and which are the stronghold of my entire existence—my language.

George Orwell's dystopian *1984* envisioned "Newspeak," the only language growing smaller every year. However, in context, its amassed connotations and propaganda tendencies only made life more difficult. Without immediately sacrificing the structure or contents of speech, I would first eliminate pronouns, acronyms, and slang as being entirely redundant. While that door is open, proper nouns used to replace their generic forms in a sort of synchronized universal synecdoche lose their flair. The days of saying Band-Aid™ when one means: "adhesive disposable bandage" will not be missed. Assuming English as our *lingua franca*, it is then a short flight to the disappearance of phrases in foreign languages affected for a pretentiously learned flair. Rounding out this first cut of oddball phrases, I wave goodbye to idioms as being too confusing to non-native speakers; onomatopoeia for being difficult to decipher without being read aloud numerous times; jargon, bureaucrat-ese and other such double-talk as being limited in range; and allusions to pop culture as being, while entertaining, thoroughly useless.

From this relatively safe vantage, the decisions become tougher, with broader ramifications. Although the adjustment would be difficult, of what real use is a name? Ruling them as entirely arbitrary, their time is next. After all, prisoners and basketball players are referred to by numbers, so why not I? That logic simultaneously wipes out the need for most proper nouns, including, but not limited to, cities, states, dates, bodies of water, and Civil War battles. What cannot be replaced with numbers is fair game for pictures. At the risk of turning the world into a round of Pictionary™, all concrete nouns and adjectives may be purged and the resultant void filled with pictures to express one's point. Simplified expression of concrete verbs is tantamount to crude charades. Loss of the whole pluperfect tense is easily accommodated by utilizing a verbal timeline with regular conjugation in past tense; sloppy speaking has rendered the subjunctive mood all but obsolete anyway. Depending on one's feelings regarding philosophy and normatively, intangible nouns and verbs, as well as morally indicative modifiers may already have been struck from the general vernacular, and so I hereby expedite the process as not strictly vital to survival. Numerals may be expressed on the fingers (with some help from scientific notation and a vote of confidence to the base ten system), while abstract adjectives are judgmental and might avoid expression altogether. We are left with little more than article adjectives and conjunctions—seemingly unnecessary in this new context, and so similarly axed. How satisfying.

In truth, this radical simplification of one's verbal databank may seem extreme, over-the-edge, horrifying; it could well be all of these things. Why not? Language is the key to self-definition and social interaction. Nonetheless, these revisions are simplifying and serve the goal of communication. With children in foreign countries or when we are just at a loss for words, we are often reduced to similar circumstances and happily find the most fundamental blocks of communication still intact. Clearing aside centuries of verbal adornment, who we are and what we do still shines through our actions, which is why the most important words survive: to be. What has been, is, and will be are the inalienable considerations made through language and so the only possessions worth fighting for. In spite of his comparative riches, Thoreau would be hard-pressed to disagree.

—Kat Lewin

COMMENTS: A word lover's dream, this essay plays with language and logic and satire and sanctimony. The writer is clearly pulling the reader's leg, and yet the tug is very enticing. For an essay like this, the reader suspends his disbelief and goes with the flow, enjoying the absurdity of it all; for underneath, the writer makes some very valid points.

Beginning with a challenge to a literary icon, the writer boldly rebukes Thoreau as she begins her argument for true simplification—her language. Each successive point of the essay builds on this premise—exaggerating and reducing language to absurd levels. She supports her points intellectually (George Orwell) and specifically (Band-Aid), but it is her whimsy that reveals her personality (*I wave goodbye to idioms*).

Now her extraordinary diction and syntax run wild, heaping image and idea upon every conceivable grammatical reference. Her abundant imagination and quirky logic impress us with their originality, and we are quite exhausted trying to keep up—hardly an illustration for simplification. And then the writer does indeed follow her own advice and simplify—*to be*—the only true possession worth fighting for.

The essay succeeds because of the unique glimpse it affords into the mind of the writer. Her complex thoughts and associations certainly indicate an advanced thinker.

Stanford University thought so, too.

EXAMPLE FIVE: FACING A CHALLENGE

I stood in front of the class—my eight-year-old hands shaking, my bottom lip quivering. I opened my mouth to speak. Nothing came out. My mouth was dry. I could not stop trembling. I practiced this presentation on Louisa May Alcott a million and one times, but now my mind was a blank. The room was spinning, and my heart was skipping beats. I attempted speech again. A shaky breath came out, a stammering voice. All I could focus on were the twenty-two pairs of eyes waiting to pounce, to rabidly devour my flesh, waiting for me to make a mistake.

I am shy. I pronounce it like a death sentence; I confess it like a sin. There is no doubt that shyness is debilitating and maladaptive in modern society, but I, as an introverted individual often feel unfairly judged by our culture. My shyness is often mistaken for moodiness, quirkiness, aloofness, or conservatism, while, in fact, I cannot help being shy anymore than someone else can help having brown eyes or freckles. What most people do not understand is introversion is not a temporary condition or mood. Rather, it is a permanent personality trait. But, what I have learned in my seventeen years is that timidity is neither the punishment nor the transgression I once believed it was.

As a child, envy would bloom bright and green whenever my sister, loquacious and gregarious, would casually and unthinkingly talk to anyone and everyone who came her way. Why couldn't I do that? Shyness overcame me like a crashing ocean wave every time I even had to answer the phone. Timidity made everything more difficult. I would constantly worry about small issues, especially where I believed I made a mistake. For every thought that a non-shy person would have, I would have twenty or thirty deliberations, worrying and reliving the hurts, the loves, the hates, the ins, the ups, the downs, the big things, the little things, the every-things, the nothings.

Yet, I am fortunate enough to have my temperament swing on a delicate pendulum, always balancing itself out. For whatever coyness my body encloses, my soul, heart, and mind attack it with spewing venom in the form of determination, stubbornness, ambition, wit, and drive. I refuse to let timidity prevail. Like two enemies in constant battle, shyness constantly clashes with other aspects of my temperament. Unfortunately, sometimes, it does triumph, and I surrender to sending an e-mail rather than picking up the telephone, or I fail to give my opinion in English class.

However, I always wrestle my timidity with the same passion, conviction, and stubbornness I use to wage war with all other challenges and impediments in my life. I may be shy, but I do not shy away from challenges that can become complicated or messy. I am never afraid of working hard, and if my introversion means working twice as much on everything in life, I will give ten times as much and toil ten times harder. For me, there is no option; there is no surrender.

Although, for the past three summers, it would have been easier for me to work at the day camp where five of my closest friends were spending their summers, I did not want to do this. Instead, I spent three to four weeks doing what I feared most—venturing like a lone pilgrim into the great unknown where I did not know a soul. I struggled with fear each time I introduced myself to someone new, and I fought each time I made a friend, resisting the temptation, the easy retreat into myself. But I did it anyway. My hands still shake and tremble whenever I have to run a meeting as co-manager of the school's public relations magazine, and my body tenses when I have to speak in front of large groups of people as an officer of the Spanish Honor Society. But I do it anyway. Part of me protests and bucks every time I answer the phone or raise my hand in class. But I will continue to do it anyway.

I will never be cured; I will always be shy. Yet, I have come to believe shyness is a strength to build on, not a character flaw to be stamped out. For, without it, I would not be as independent as I am or have the few extraordinary close friends that I do. I would never have discovered my passion and love for writing or my salvation in reading. I would have never felt the need to investigate my temperament or the curiosity to study the effects of shyness on myself and others, both of which led to my Intel project on behavioral inhibition and its relation to anxiety; without the introspection that shyness provides, I may have never completed any such study or project at all. Without introversion, my life would be different; *I* would be different. Although there are times when I wish I could simply get up and control the room without my lip quivering and legs wobbling, or chat with any group of strangers without reservation or hesitation, I have come to embrace and accept my other personality traits—my determination, my wit, my ambition. As Charlotte Brontë said, "If we had no winter, the spring would not be so pleasant: if we did not sometimes taste adversity, prosperity would not be so welcome." My achievement comes not by denying shyness, but occasionally, by setting it aside and letting pride and perspiration come first. And then, when success comes, it is that much more of a triumph.

I stand in front of the class, my seventeen-year-old hands slightly shaking. Calm down, I tell myself. You know this, you know you do. I try not to focus on the twenty-two pairs of eyes. Come on, I urge myself. You can do this. I repeat the mantra over and over again. I open my mouth to speak. Loudly, clearly, as if by sheer will, the words flow out...

—Allison Ivans

COMMENTS: This essay reflects the art of a wonderful writer, one who obviously loves words. Her introduction and conclusion frame the essay and chronicle her growth. The length of the sentences in the intro creates the panic and tension the speaker feels and sets the stage for the reflective nature of the body. The essay, an analysis of a personality trait, gleams with insight. *Timidity is neither the punishment nor the transgression I once believed it was; I may be shy, but I do not shy away from challenges; I have come to believe shyness is a strength to build on, not a character flaw to be stamped out.*

In the body of the essay, the writer includes details that would otherwise be mundane but for her skill. She reveals her achievements—honor society, Intel project, magazine manager, summer job, by linking them to her understanding the power of her shyness. Her diction is vivid and precise: *debilitating and maladaptive; loquacious and gregarious; deliberations; delicate pendulum; spewing venom; lip quivering and legs wobbling.*

But it is the imagery and metaphoric language that raise the essay to its level of promise and excellence. Comparisons abound, enlivening the writing. *Like a death sentence; I confess it like a sin; envy would bloom bright and green; shyness overcame me like a crashing ocean wave; like two enemies in constant battle, shyness constantly clashes with other aspects of my temperament.*

The words flow out...and the reader listens!

☞ YOUR TURN ☜

Examine a trait you may possess which might be construed as a negative, and illustrate it in a positive manner.

Deliberately edit an essay you have been working on, and infuse it with metaphoric language. Play with this. If, when you've finished, you feel that the result is awkward or trite, remove the metaphors and other poetic language you have added. However, you may be surprised to find that one interesting simile can spark your writing and open new avenues for you to pursue.

Recheck your essay to eliminate tired words and images, and substitute vigorous, active, and precise ones. Be careful not to fall into the thesaurus trap. Use a thesaurus for ideas, but be sure you understand the subtleties and connotations of the words you choose.

EXAMPLE SIX: PERSONAL IDENTITY

"The Road Not Taken"

Often we had Sunday brunch at my uncle's Shanghai place on the bend where Canal meets Lafayette. It was on the border where Soho violently transitions into Chinatown, and if I stood at the entryway, I could turn in opposite directions and experience two infinitely different scenes.

"Two roads diverged in a wood, and I—"

To my right there was the homogeneity of an East Asian culture, a pageant of foreign characters and a swarm of exotic scents. To my left was the potpourri of many worlds, cultures so entwined that none seemed to command. After lunch, my cousins and brother would always venture right, and into the heart of Chinatown. As I was drawn towards the left, the alien scents of ginger and star anise would grow fainter in the background, and I would start to feel a little more comfortable. I would never look back.

"Two roads diverged in a wood, and I—

I took the one less traveled by,"

I have always been the odd-ball in the family—the rebel, the non-conformist. When my family gathered to celebrate the Chinese New Year, I was attending confirmation, reading the *Haggadah* at Passover, and celebrating Pascha or Greek Easter. It seems illogical and unnatural for me to immerse myself in but one culture considering I had been nurtured around so many. Eating Chinese moon cakes during Mid-Autumn festival seems just as natural to me as lighting the Menorah on the first night of Chanukah. I was; I am: always will be the product of my environment—much to the incredulity of my parents.

Just the other day, my mother remarked in that dogmatic tone of hers, "Why can't you just be Asian?" An argument ensued. I asked, "What is an Asian? Do I have slanty eyes; a great work ethic? Should I eat Chinese food all day; how about I speak with a foreign accent? Would that make me Asian, Mom?" Once, while visiting a nursing home, a man had refused to talk to me because I, "had bombed Pearl Harbor." Clearly I, as an Asian, was personally a catalyst for the US entry into the Second World War.

According to my family, everyone was catalogued as either Asian or non-Asian. I was clearly that duck for which my parents were not prepared. I had simply waddled astray from that neat and structured brick path that they had laid for me; all our interactions were merely a chance for them to reeducate and guide me back onto that correct route. Little did they know that I had no intention of returning to that sheltered nest they had prepared. The self-segregation that they wished me to adopt was simply not what I sought. That it made them comfortable was one thing, but my comfort zone resides in the amalgamation of many cultures— my horizons are so much more enticing.

Yes, I am Asian; but, I am Italian, Greek, and Irish as well; I am also Jewish, Catholic, and an atheist. I am not a single ethnicity, religion, nor anyone's expectation; I am not a stereotype. I am who I am. I am Neil Chen, no more, no less.
"Two roads diverged in a wood, and I—

I took the one less traveled by,

And that has made all the difference."

Quotations and ideas adapted from Robert Frost's poem "The Road Not Taken."

—Neil Chen

COMMENTS: Wow, the intro says it all! Look at how the diction creates the theme of the essay: *On the bend where Canal meets Lafayette, on the border where Soho violently transitions into Chinatown, I stood at the entryway, turn, opposite directions, two infinitely different.* There is nothing extraneous—every image and phrase points to the conflict faced by the writer. And this opening also reveals the skill and control of the writer. This is a mature and deliberate thinker at work.

He continues to set the stage with exotic details, placing himself in the middle of the mélange of cultural experiences he considers alien. The diminishing *scents of ginger and star anise* echo his diminishing connection with his traditional roots.

The remainder of the essay illustrates his contention that *I have always been the odd-ball in the family.* In so doing, he shares his breadth of individuality and the obstacles he faces in a world that does not yet appreciate, as he does, the *amalgamation of many cultures.* A wider horizon beckons the writer, and he responds. His final paragraph, whose form and effect depend on the repetition of the words *I am,* clearly reflects his credo.

Part of what sets this essay apart from the ordinary is the clever embedding of Frost's poem at the appropriate points of the essay: first to state the conflict, then to indicate the choice, and finally to emphasize the result. It has indeed *made all the difference.*

Openings

As you learned in Chapter 4, whether explicit or implicit, there is a wide range of openings possible. Each of these introductions has a certain charm that engages the reader.

Read the following openings and the commentaries to see if you can use any of the techniques as a springboard for your own essay.

EXAMPLE ONE: USING STATISTICS

S.S. # 000-00-000. 1390 SAT. 30 ACT. 87 G.P.A. 8/14/86 D.O.B. LB#24 BASS 1

These numbers and letters are all used to identify me, and at this point, are the only means of identification that are available to you. Unfortunately, the numbers are barely a fair representation of who Timothy P. Gill is. In no way do these numbers say anything about the kind of person I am. They say nothing about my ambition, drive, motivation, successes and failures. Numbers don't tell about the lessons that I have learned or the experiences that have shaped and molded my life.

I am much more than a bunch of numbers.

—Timothy Gill

COMMENTS: Tim captures the frustration every applicant feels—how to distinguish oneself from the anonymous mass that has been dehumanized and reduced to a series of numerals. It is a brave beginning for an essay because it demands that the writer present his uniqueness. But it also plays right into the purpose of an application essay: the opportunity to counteract the necessary statistical information with a personal statement. Tim lives up to the challenge he sets.

EXAMPLE TWO: ENGAGING DETAILS

Cruising at night in a silver Ford Contour, singing off key with four of my best friends...eating Taco Bell and giggling about what a fool I made out of myself earlier that day. Sitting in math class, laughing as Mr. Reed makes another one of his sarcastic remarks...finding out I am the captain of the field hockey team... scoring two goals in a field hockey game and then later that night finding I am homecoming queen. Life is good.

—Brooke Nielsen

COMMENTS: Engaging and easy to identify with, this opening has the sweetness of nostalgia and the enthusiasm of its current reality. The reader senses that this is a sensitive applicant who is well aware of the joy of simple pleasures and at the same time is part of creating those delights. Her upbeat tone and subsequent illustrations reveal a well-balanced and grounded candidate.

EXAMPLE THREE: A CHALLENGE

I was stuck. I was stuck in a lifestyle of sameness, repetition and security. Why I changed doesn't really matter. How I changed doesn't really matter. What really matters is the outcome. Waking up every morning with the same routine made me feel safe.

But it was time for the routine to take a rest. I was ready to wake up in the morning a new me. I did not want to know what would happen next. I wanted the unknown.

—Nicole Tsourovakas

COMMENTS: The writer matches her style to her meaning. She uses parallelism and repetition to reinforce the idea of sameness, cleverly illustrating the routine. She plays with opposition: *waking* and *rest*, *knowing* and *not knowing,* and *wanting* and *not wanting*. Her diction is simple, but her control is complex.

EXAMPLE FOUR: CONTRAST FOR EFFECT

I've mourned the loss of a goldfish and the loss of a grandmother. I've studied for math tests and failed regardless. I've purchased lottery tickets; I'm still not a millionaire. I've fought with my sisters, been defeated in tennis matches, and I once lost a student council election. I've been chosen last for kickball; I've wept the loss of my long time teacher, coach and friend. I've lost races in the mud; I've lost hoola-hoop contests, but I've never lost the ability to smile and appreciate life.

—Danielle Labadorf

COMMENTS: This ingenious introduction, one that many can identify with, is effective because of its use of antithesis. The writer sets herself up as the quintessential loser and then contradicts her assertion with the key to her personality: her ability to smile and appreciate life. By juxtaposing the trivial with the significant, she manages to enumerate many of her experiences while tempering the emotional details. The contrapuntal effect of the serious and the humorous is pleasing and engaging.

☞ YOUR TURN ☜

Consider using contrast to create an anecdote or description. Mix images and details of varying importance to make your point. Often, a minor episode can be the catalyst for a major insight.

EXAMPLE FIVE: QUOTATION

As Ingmar Bergman once said, "No art passes our conscience in the way film does, and goes directly to our feelings, deep down into the dark rooms of our souls." Bergman certainly hit the nail on the head. Throughout my life, I see parts of myself in the characters on the big screen. A little bit of Lloyd from *Say Anything* reflects my hopeless romantic side, a little bit of Tyler Durden from *Fight Club* reveals my existentialist side, and even a little bit of Charles Foster Kane from *Citizen Kane*, portrays the side of me wishing for an uncomplicated life, a way to go back to the past. As I move toward the future, the more I see that I should be my own character. I should be me, and make what I want of myself.

—Kaveh Tabatabaie

COMMENTS: An effective opening invites the reader in. This one has the advantage of an engaging topic—the movies. The writer expresses himself through his choice of examples, and he chooses a diverse sampling to tempt the reader to learn more about him. The quotation adds a touch of scholarship and direction and is referenced later in the body of the essay, while the final sentence of the paragraph reinforces the decisiveness and direction of the writer.

☞ YOUR TURN ☜

Consider your favorite movie characters (or literary ones) and develop an analogous relationship between you and the role. Discuss yourself in light of the persona you've chosen. Provide several concrete points of comparison or disparity.

EXAMPLE SIX: A STARTLING STATEMENT

The new millennium, 2000, was anything but ordinary. My dog became deaf. My brother moved out. My sister left public school for Catholic school. My father permanently moved to Maryland. My mother became a lesbian.

—Arielle Laurie

COMMENTS: This very personal essay takes a risk and handles a sensitive subject in a mature and honest manner. The opening paragraph is striking in its development. Each statement is self-contained, matter-of-fact, and final. The cadence, with its parallelism, is wonderful, rushing the reader into an unexpected progression deliberately staged for effect and building to the most challenging change faced. Her subsequent paragraphs reveal the writer's actions and reactions.

EXAMPLE SEVEN: VIVID DETAILS

I sit down on the sheet-covered couch and sink like a brick in water. As I lean over my plate, just able to reach over the surface of the table, I realize the remarkable feat that has just been accomplished: a family of 12 squeezing around a table made for 6 with just enough room to move one's elbows. The man sitting at the head of the table in his plastic lawn chair is my grandfather. He's in his early 80's, having survived the Great Depression, World War II, and triple by-pass surgery. He's the youngest in a family of native Greeks. His face, gentle and serene, reminds me of the purity of a child, a paradox when I consider the extreme turmoil surrounding his life. His bottom lip is always protruding over the upper portion and his pants are enormous in comparison to his tiny waist. He's been retired for 10 years now, spending his days walking his 2 dogs, watching TV, and making weekly trips to the supermarket. My grandmother, the daughter of Hungarian parents, had a similar life to that of my grandfather. Both grew up in the Bronx among clusters of immigrants, surviving both periods of wars and periods of peace together as a community. Now, their community long dispersed, they are alone.

—Rachel Beller

COMMENTS: This opening evokes the time and place of the subject of the essay. The writer pays careful attention to detail but does not romanticize her portrait. She succeeds in setting the stage for a touching portrait of her grandparents and, ultimately, of herself.

Closings

An effective conclusion leaves the reader with a sense of closure. It has the reader saying, "Oh, I see," or "Great last line." It also can leave the reader with:

➤ A smile

➤ A sense of satisfaction

➤ An insight

➤ A lump in the throat

➤ An appreciation of the writer as a person

EXAMPLE ONE: QUOTATION

Change is a fact of life. That is what growing is all about. "If we don't change, we don't grow. If we don't grow, we aren't living"—Gail Sheehy. I'm ready to live and grow. Entering college is a change in life that will open many new doors for me. A new chapter in my life will be opened. I'm ready to experience the unexpected. I'm ready to take on the future with a positive attitude and live a life full of change and new faces.

—Nicole Tsourovakas

COMMENTS: This ending is strengthened by the inclusion of an appropriate quotation that underscores the writer's purpose. She links her final thoughts to the opening concepts of known and unknown, security and change. It is a solid and clear statement.

EXAMPLE TWO: INSIGHT

Aldous Huxley said, "Experience is not what happens to you, it's what you do with what happens to you." As senior year has come around, I realize that I have changed my view of my life and my choices. Sometimes life throws curve-balls, like divorce, and life-style changes, and gaining a step-mom through a same sex-relationship. We are given a choice about how to react. I chose to step up to the plate with an open mind and learn something about the trajectory of that ball.

—Arielle Laurie

COMMENTS: The writer chooses a very appropriate quotation to begin her conclusion as she applies it to her own experience. Arielle's decision introduced earlier in her essay to accept the choices in her life with open-mindedness and wisdom makes the reader want to shout, "Way to go!"

EXAMPLE THREE: INSIGHT

This experience has allowed me to learn the importance of the philosophy, "live life to the fullest." When I was becoming a bar mitzvah, my rabbi said to me, *Ari, look around and remember everything about this moment—who is here and why they came here. In years to come, you will appreciate this more than anything.* I still have a vivid image of that moment and because of the emotion that image evokes, I try to live in the present as often as possible. This is because, years from now, I hope to be able to look back at the challenges of Yale and say, "Wow, I wish I could do that again."

—Ari Allen

COMMENTS: This conclusion, which follows an explanation of a service project the writer initiated, is interesting because it does not seem to grow from the essay. However, it does allude to the essence of the essay, the lesson learned through initiative and hard work. The writer equates his insight with a highly emotional and personal moment in his life and then links this emotion to his college aspirations.

EXAMPLE FOUR: INSIGHT

The visits I have with my grandparents are, and will continue to be, the most enriching history lessons I have encountered. Their words bring to life the facts in my textbooks. They are an invaluable source of information to me as I am their source of companionship. They may no longer have the close-knit friends of their childhood, but I provide them with the same listening ear and eager interest. There may no longer be a street stoop for them to sit on and gossip or a sidewalk to gather on with their friends, but there's a sunken-in couch, in a small house in New Jersey, where they have a grandchild with whom to share all their experiences and thoughts.

—Rachel Beller

COMMENTS: A very nice wrap-up for the essay—one that lovingly delineates the relationship and reveals the writer's warmth and insight.

EXAMPLE FIVE : ANECDOTE

So there I was, standing in front of an enormous crowd, my palms sweating, my breath coming out short and labored. Summoning up my courage (what little I had), I began to sing. Now, I'm not going to tell you that I went up on that stage and sang the best solo of my life, with everyone applauding and asking me for an encore, and just like that POOF! my stage fright was gone. Actually, far from it. It was probably close to the worst four minutes of my life. My voice kept cracking and at one point I actually forgot my words. But, once I got off the stage the feeling was incredible. Aside from relief which was pretty prominent, I felt overwhelming pride. I had conquered my fear. It was truly one of my proudest moments.

—Chrissy Makris

COMMENTS: This final paragraph, which presents the moment of triumph over a fear, is effective because it is so honest. The writer does not offer a candy-coated transformation. Instead, she is realistic, self-deprecating, and endearingly human. It is this sincerity mixed with the exultation she feels that creates such a positive impression of the applicant.

EXAMPLE SIX: A LOOK TO THE FUTURE

I remember when you didn't want to wear shoes to school," my mother wistfully reminisced as I tried on a new pair of Steve Maddens during our annual back-to-school shopping jaunt. I laughed to myself because the memory is etched in my mind. Only now I genuinely understand why being barefoot means more than its simple act. It symbolizes my progressiveness, my self-assurance, my capability, my preference and my sense of independence, all the while reminding me that there will be rocks along the way. Strolling barefoot through my newly cultivated field, my toes neatly adorned with a French pedicure, I consider what college will be like as I aspire towards my goal of being a dentist one day. As I contemplate the future, my inner voice reassures me of my barefooted farm girl spirit; it speaks of my sovereignty and the freedoms I keenly embrace. Sure-footed, I am ready to take a risk with each new step.

—Virginia Viviano

COMMENTS: Reflecting the observations of the writer, this closing paragraph works because it ties up the previous paragraphs: the paper had opened with a barefoot child and now ends with a college applicant in new shoes. The paper had explored a farm that needed weeding and planting, and it concludes with a newly cultivated field, a metaphor for the writer herself. The two sides of the writer are revealed, the young sophisticate and the farm girl. Her transition complete, the lessons of the farm learned, the speaker acknowledges her own growth—*sure-footed* and *ready to take a risk*. College is ready for her, too.

Sparkling Bits and Pieces

Sometimes the uniqueness of the writer is conveyed not by the big picture (the complete essay) but rather in a sentence, a phrase, a paragraph, or an image. The following bits and pieces from student essays grab the reader and elevate the essays from static to dynamic.

EXAMPLE ONE: USING IMAGERY AND CONTRAST

Look carefully at these excerpts from two different paragraphs in the body of this student's essay.

I no longer valued the ripples over my fingertips as I dragged them along the silky surface. I began to dread the water, as knots tightened in my stomach and my mouth became desert dry before a race. Thoughts of quitting ran through my head, but letting the team down was not an option. So, I stuck with the team, attending practices and meets with a smiling façade....

The passion I have developed for the oboe has also given me the opportunity to succeed, retaining my section leader status for nine years and playing solos in concert band. I love running my fingers along the silver keys, transforming the once duck-like clatter into a kitten's purr.

—Julie Kaplan

COMMENTS: This strong essay begins with an athletic challenge and shifts to an artistic performance. The sentences above are effective for their imagery and contrast. It is interesting to see the change in the writer's focus as she maintains drive, determination, and commitment while moving from a physical plane to a mental one.

EXAMPLE TWO: A STARTLING METAPHOR

As I become increasingly nostalgic about past stories I have written in elementary school, I conversely become increasingly depressed as I reflect on all the drudge I have written over the past three years. Now, don't get me wrong, this was not necessarily bad writing...it was just bad to write. English has conveniently been turning into math, where formulas and templates have taken over ideas and creativity. When I wrote as a youth, I felt much like a mosquito in a nudist colony—so much to do and no idea where to begin. But the spark has left me, and the fuel that got me into AP English class is forever stagnant.

—Jake Rosenblum

COMMENTS: Clever and on the mark, this essay flirts with danger. The writer tells us, in a tongue-in-cheek tone that nonetheless hits home, that he has endured *years of grueling essays*. It is his humor that wins the reader. *Now don't get me wrong, this was not necessarily bad writing...it was just bad to write. English has conveniently been turning into math, where formulas and templates have taken over ideas and creativity.* The reader is probably sighing in agreement.

The writer's wit is evident as he metaphorically bemoans the loss of *the spark* and *the fuel*. It is obvious that he is still brightly shining as evidenced by sentences such as *I felt much like a mosquito in a nudist colony—so much to do and no idea where to begin.* This writer knew exactly where to begin, and the remainder of his essay proves it.

EXAMPLE THREE: USING A NARRATIVE

The boys did like me, despite their mean-hearted jokes, but they'd always keep me under tight watch. One wrong move and the mockery would be unleashed. *You dropped it! Ha, Ha! You know why? Tell her boys! Because you're a gi-rl!* My usual response was, *Wow. In all seriousness, that one never gets old. And, I especially like the singsong tone it has now. Clive Davis should be contacting you all real soon.* So, I'd ignore them as usual, pick up the ball, and keep playing. I'd say nothing if one of the boys dropped the ball, being the mature 8-year-old I was. All right, maybe I laughed a little to myself, a little too loud, for a little too long, no biggie. But, please, by age 8 I already knew of the crazy societal stereotypes and let me tell you, I was unimpressed. I'd had enough of their *I am man, hear me roar.* I was girl. I could roar—just as loud.

—Stephanie Bragman

COMMENTS: The reader can certainly hear the voice of the writer roar. She has an ear for genuine dialogue, and the anecdote rings true. Her natural sense of humor and lighthearted tone are appropriate for presenting the way in which she approached the gender wars of youth. Here is a candidate who rolls with the punches and refuses to live by unfair rules. We'd choose her to play on our team, too.

Relate an episode from childhood that was pivotal in its impact. Narrow your focus to a dialogue between you and others. Re-create the conversation linking it to an aspect of your development or personality.

EXAMPLE FOUR: USE OF DETAILS AND IMAGERY

My muscles are tense, as the gun is poised in the air, ready to spark the explosion of shouts and exclamations of encouragement from this presently apprehensive, quiet atmosphere. With a sharp bang, a multitude of colors representing each school spills over the line like the emptying of a bag of Skittles onto the field. Entering the familiar course I know I have to hug the curves and use the downhills, but these measures seem to cause little advantage. Heavy footsteps and labored breathing approach from behind on the right side. The maddening tempo has a surprisingly mellowing impact. The beat is hypnotic until I can put a name to the rhythm, that blur of blue, East Meadow. The girl maneuvers herself so she takes up stride right beside me. I stay with her. There is no way I'm going to lose to this girl after all I've put into my training.

—Meredith Maus

COMMENTS: Sharp details, sensory imagery, and poetic devices combine to recreate the cross-country experience of the writer. The writing is as focused as the athlete—there are no extraneous words to detract from the single effect of the paragraph on the reader.

This is a fine example of "show, don't tell." We feel the energy and the commitment of the writer as she competes with her rival and herself.

By the way, although this was part of the body of the essay, it could as easily have been an opening paragraph.

☞ YOUR TURN ☜

Show the reader a tense situation you have experienced. Write about something you know well, and through diction, syntax, and imagery, re-create the moment.

EXAMPLE FIVE: A MEMORY OF THE PAST

Though I never really excelled at many activities (to this day I still don't understand the point of dodge ball), I knew I could do one thing better than anyone else, and that was read. So, while my classmates were busy reading "Clifford, the Big Red Dog" and listening to books on tape, I liked the more insightful books, the deeper books...*The Babysitters Club*. Yes, I know, *The Babysitters Club*, you ask? It may sound a bit inane, but *The Babysitters Club* taught me invaluable lessons. As a young girl I loved to read about the lives of the club and pretend I was one of the girls. I strove to be like Claudia, outgoing, funny, talented and popular. Though I have long since outgrown those books, the lessons I learned from them still remain with me to this day. Never leave a child unattended, starting a babysitters club is not as easy as it sounds (trust me, we've all tried it), and most importantly, never attempt to change who you are to fit in. Whenever I have a conflict I don't know how to handle, I still find myself thinking, what would a member of the club do?

—Chrissy Makris

COMMENTS: This informal and chatty paragraph illustrates part of a meaningful structure for the essay. This first body paragraph reveals the young reader, and subsequent paragraphs will evolve and mature, as did the author. It is clever of the writer to begin the body with her young tastes in reading. She engages the reader with her rhetorical questions and parenthetical phrases. These allow her to comment on her own choice of detail and examples. She establishes a warm and thoughtful tone and uses her final sentence to remind the reader that she relies on past lessons and is ready to move to the next paragraph and insight.

EXAMPLE SIX: AN ANECDOTE

By the 1000 meter mark some of the other crews had passed us, and we were sitting in fifth place. Hitting the 750 meter mark we still sat in a tight 5th right behind the 4th place boat. My hands were molded on the ore handles. My eyes were fixed on my teammate in front of me. Nothing could distract me. I was in the zone. Realizing that the race was almost over, we kicked it up. My muscles bulged and my skin was drenched in sweat; the four of us pushed past the point of pain. We still had 250 meters left. We moved up and passed another boat putting us in 4th place and the stern of the third place boat was right on our bow. We had only 100 meters at this point. My vision was blurred and my hearing faint. However, I was still pulling with a stroke rating that felt as if we were flying. We took that last stroke when we heard the faded sound of the buzzer. The boat went silent. No one spoke. It wasn't that we were upset; it was the pure fact that we couldn't talk. We had pushed it so hard for that seven or so minutes that there was nothing left. We had emptied the tank. It took us longer to row the 200 meters to the dock than it did for us to row the whole course.

—Ashleigh Tate

COMMENTS: The deliberately short, choppy syntax highlights the tension and the exhaustion the writer feels. It is as if she must gulp for the words and conserve her energy for rowing. With strong verbs, metaphors and similes, and sensory imagery, the writer takes the reader along for the race. Her determination, commitment and teamwork are clearly evident.

EXAMPLE SEVEN: USING IRONY

I was the living symbol of Hollywood cinema: *The Mighty Ducks, Bad News Bears* and *Hardball*. I was the unknown—the newcomer to the position of coaching. As the last resort and last hope of Boys and Girls Club, I agreed to coach the fifth grade girl's basketball team. How could I conduct a practice, make a winning team, prove everyone else wrong and teach these girls the importance of the game? Was there a book *Coaching for Dummies* that I could read?

—Kathleen Kenary

COMMENTS: By making references to well-known films, this student invites the reader to share her feelings. The clever and obviously deliberate reference to the famous (or infamous) *Dummies* book series also shows the writer's humility and sense of humor. The reader is going to be on her side throughout the essay.

EXAMPLE EIGHT: USING AN EXTENDED METAPHOR

So, here I am, an enigma on the way to being solved. I am that 17-year-old senior staring at her future; that 17-year-old senior who went from quiet to "Funniest" in her senior class. I went from extremely self-conscious to confident, from inhibited to gregarious. The questions of "how" or "why" this change occurred I find hard to answer. The "what" and the "who" questions are a lot easier....

I am a painting you look at a second time. I am a Salvador Dali—quirky and strange, but at the same time provocative and interesting. I am a Claude Monet— serene and colorful but lively and substantial. I am a cluster of colors that generally add up to a vibrant but sensitive picture.

—Michala Smith

COMMENTS: Here is a writer who truly has a sense of herself, and that personal identity is vividly portrayed with her self-comparisons to different, well-known paintings of both surrealist and impressionist artists. Her creative nature is apparent to the reader.

☞ YOUR TURN ☜

Describe yourself in terms of works of art, music, dance, etc. Try for a specific style such as romantic, impressionistic, rock, jazz, improv, classical, rap, or hip-hop. Or compare yourself to natural images: animals, water, mountains. You get the idea—think quirky; pull out all the stops and play.

EXAMPLE NINE: VIVID DETAILS AND ANALOGIES

On the day of the parade, I arrived at the school's parking lot for the beginning of the festivities. I saw our five foot by three foot platform with a black crêpe paper coffin measuring about four feet by two feet, damp, soggy and falling apart because the senior class had sprayed it with a hose the night before, and our four characters that almost defied description. The southern gentleman was a boy wearing a four sizes too big tattered corduroy suit he picked up at a thrift store and a straw hat. He looked more like an Appalachian moonshiner than Colonel Sanders. At least he put in effort though which was more than I could say for our southern lady who put on her sister's prom dress and carried an umbrella. The saxophone player did actually have a sax, but his outfit—a black suit, white shirt, black tie, sunglasses and fedora hat—made him look like Elwood Blues. Our voodoo priestess apparently misunderstood the concept of voodoo; she looked more like a New Orleans streetwalker. The only clue to her true identity was the rubber chicken smeared with ketchup she carried in tow.

Just when I thought it could not get any more ludicrous, our towing vehicle arrived. It was a Ford Expedition. Being twice as wide and four times as long, it completely dwarfed our float. However, the homecoming parade waits for no man, and soon the marching band struck up its tune, confetti flew, and people cheered as the patriotic Boston float and the 1920's Hollywood float pulled out ahead of us. Behind us was the hippie San Francisco float. And, there, in the third slot, was our float, black and morbid, looking not like the French Quarter-Jazz-Riverboat-Genteel image we had wanted, but more like *Rocky Horror*'s funeral procession.

—Erin Brown

COMMENTS: The subject of this essay is learning from past mistakes about building a homecoming float. The body of the essay contains several examples of vivid details and highly visual metaphors, such as *The saxophone player did actually have a sax, but his outfit—a black suit, white shirt, black tie, sunglasses and fedora hat—made him look like Elwood Blues. Our voodoo priestess apparently misunderstood the concept of voodoo; she looked more like a New Orleans streetwalker. The only clue to her true identity was the rubber chicken smeared with ketchup she carried in tow. And, there, in the third slot, was our float, black and morbid, looking not like the French Quarter-Jazz-Riverboat-Genteel image we had wanted, but more like* Rocky Horror's *funeral procession.*

The reader not only sees this sorry excuse for a float but also gets a very real sense of the writer's sense of humor, irony, and determination.

AFTERWORD

♥ Congratulations! You've reached the finish line. Some of you have just thumbed through the book and pinpointed what's available to you. Others have read and spent time with certain sections and skimmed the remaining material. And a percentage of you have faithfully read and been involved with the activities from page one through to these last pages.

You've done what you thought was best for you and by now have completed one or more of the following:

☑ Your own personal interview.

☑ The first draft of your application essay(s).

☑ Evaluation and revision of your first draft.

☑ Preparations to send off your essay to the college(s) to which you are applying.

What follows is a checklist that you may wish to use now that you have worked your way through the application essay process.

I have:

_____ Made a list of colleges I would like to attend

_____ Looked at the catalogue for each college

_____ Perused the Web site of each college

_____ Spoken to my parents about my choices

_____ Spoken to my guidance counselor about my choices

_____ Spoken with college reps and people who have attended each college

_____ Sent for and received the necessary college application forms

_____ Conducted my own personal interview

_____ Chosen two or three items from the personal interview that really hit home with me

_____ Prepared the brief notes on each of the chosen items

For each essay that I wrote, I have:

_____ Written my first draft

_____ Made certain that I project a clear voice

_____ Considered what the subtext (reading between the lines) says about me

_____ Had someone read it aloud to me

_____ Evaluated my first draft (____mechanics; ____content; ____length)

_____ Written my revision

_____ Had someone read the revision aloud to me

_____ Made any needed final adjustments to the revised essay

_____ Printed out the final draft of my essay

_____ Had someone read the final draft aloud to me *before* submitting it

I must be certain to:

_____ Do a final proofread

_____ Match the essay with the appropriate college in the appropriate envelope

_____ Check that I have written the short-response essays if they were required

_____ Submit the application BEFORE the deadline

_____ Put the proper postage on the envelope

We wish you insightful thoughts, smooth transitions, and positive responses.

ABOUT THE AUTHORS

ESTELLE RANKIN taught English at Jericho High School for over 30 years. She was honored with the AP Literature Teacher of the Year award by the College Board in 1996. She also received the Long Island Teacher of the Year award in 1990. In addition, she was the recipient of the Cornell University Presidential Scholars' award and has been recognized by the C. W. Post Master Teachers Program.

Ms. Rankin earned her BA from Adelphi University and her MA from Hofstra University. She has pursued further graduate work in the field of creative studies at Queens College and Brooklyn University. Her finest teachers were her parents, Edward and Sylvia Stern.

Ms. Rankin has done extensive work in the research and development of film, drama, and creative writing curricula and has participated in numerous AP Literature conferences and workshops. She is a consultant for Building Success and Vertical Teams and is also a literature presenter for the Advanced Placement Specialty conferences. In addition, she pioneered a senior initiative mentoring program based on internships and service and has conducted many English workshops for both teachers and students at high schools and middle schools for New York's Board of Cooperative Educational Services (B.O.C.E.S.).

BARBARA MURPHY taught English at Jericho High School for over 30 years. She has been a reader of the AP Language and Composition exam since 1993 and is a consultant for the College Board's AP Language and Composition, Pre-AP, and Building for Success divisions, for whom she has conducted workshops, conferences, specialty conference presentations, and summer institutes. Ms. Murphy is currently on the faculty of Syracuse University's Project Advance in English. After earning her BA from Duquesne University and her MA from the University of Pittsburgh, she did her doctoral course work at Columbia University. She also holds professional certifications in still photography and motion picture production and is one of the founding members of the women's film company Ishtar Films.

Ms. Murphy and Ms. Rankin are the coauthors of McGraw-Hill's *5 Steps to a 5: The AP English Language Exam*, *5 Steps to a 5: The AP English Literature Exam*, and *Writing the AP English Essay*.

Notes

Notes

Notes

Notes

Notes

Notes

Notes

Notes